PENGUIN BUSINESS

HOW COME NO ONE TOLD ME THAT?

Prakash Iyer is the bestselling author of *The Habit of Winning* and *The Secret of Leadership*. In a corporate career spanning more than three decades, he has worked with teams selling everything from soaps and colas to yellow pages and diapers. Previously, he was the managing director of Kimberly-Clark Lever. Passionate about people, Prakash is also a motivational speaker, a certified leadership coach and an uncertified cricket junkie. An alumnus of IIM Ahmedabad, he lives in Pune with his wife, Savitha.

HOW COME NO ONE TOLD ME THAT?

Life LESSONS, Practical ADVICE and Timeless WISDOM for SUCCESS

PRAKASH IYER

BUSINESS

An imprint of Penguin Random House

PENGUIN BUSINESS

USA | Canada | UK | Ireland | Australia
New Zealand | India | South Africa | China

Penguin Business is part of the Penguin Random House group of companies whose addresses can be found at global.penguinrandomhouse.com

Published by Penguin Random House India Pvt. Ltd
4th Floor, Capital Tower 1, MG Road,
Gurugram 122 002, Haryana, India

Penguin
Random House
India

First published in Portfolio by Penguin Random House India 2021
Published in Penguin Business 2023

15 14 13 12

ISBN 9780143421368

Typeset in Aldine401 BT by Manipal Technologies Limited, Manipal
Printed at Replika Press Pvt. Ltd, India

www.penguin.co.in

FSC
www.fsc.org
MIX
Paper from responsible sources
FSC® C016779

For Tuts and Abby

Contents

WHAT REALLY MATTERS

Introduction

It's funny, isn't it?

Think about it. We went through ten years of school, where we learnt about amoeba and Akbar, and how to dissect a frog and bisect an angle. We mugged up answers for exams and groaned under the weight of homework that stopped us from playing an extra fifteen minutes of French cricket, or *Mortal Kombat*.

How come no one told us to enjoy our childhood, have fun with friends and become the kind of kid everyone wants to play with?

Then we went to college, and some of us learnt how to build bridges across rivers. How come no one told us about building bridges with other people? Some of us went to business schools and learnt how to manage businesses. Alas, there were no courses on offer on how to manage our own lives.

We grew up competing. Trying to get ahead of the rest of the class. We fought to get to the front of the queue. And we grew up feeling inadequate. Because when we did not ace a test, we got branded as being not good enough.

We got ranked in class and grew up thinking, maybe, just maybe, we were not good enough. And we continued to jostle to get ahead of friends and colleagues.

How come no one told us that learning to collaborate was way more powerful than learning to compete? Or that being a good team player could be a valuable life skill? And that while good grades were nice to have, they didn't always accurately define our true potential?

It's the story of our lives. Our education teaches us a lot, but it does not quite prepare us for the larger game of life. The real lessons are often the ones we learn in the school of hard knocks. In the real world. Those are the lessons that help us learn and get better.

The book you now hold in your hands is a collection of some of the lessons I have learnt in my life. Sometimes, small, seemingly insignificant events can teach us valuable lessons. Just as sometimes chance conversations with strangers can open our eyes to powerful truths. A tiny paragraph tucked away in a book can turn on a lightbulb inside our heads. And a little nugget from a successful person's life can show us the way to creating our own success story. The problem, though, is that many of us go through our lives without having the opportunity to learn these lessons. We don't always get this advice. And in some cases, we don't pay heed to the advice because of the manner in which it is conveyed to us. Or because we did not get to hear it when we needed to. Not learning those lessons often impacts the way we think, our sense of self-worth, our ability to work with other people. And that prevents several among us from becoming the people we were meant to be.

I have been a big believer in the power of stories. Stories and storytelling have become a part of my life now. I sometimes think I am always looking at everything around me through two lenses: a normal lens and a 'what-does-this-tell-us-about-life' lens. One lens sees and absorbs what I am seeing and hearing. And the other lens seems to focus on, 'Wow, so what can we learn from this? What's the story here?' Like a compulsive punster looking for a second meaning in everything, I find myself hunting for the story behind the obvious. This might explain my tendency to draw lessons from ordinary events. And this might also explain why my wife thinks I am not listening and am lost in another world most times!

Stories are memorable. They stick in our heads and our hearts. They can inspire. And they have the ability to make us look at our lives through a very different lens. The lessons and advice in this book come to you as stories. You will find simple anecdotes, everyday events and the lessons we can learn from them. Like learning from my not-yet-five-year-old twins how we make the mistake of wanting things just because everyone seems to want them. Or how a shoelace taught me that just because we've been doing things in a certain way for many years doesn't mean we are doing it right. And lessons in fostering teamwork and building the right culture, from the lunchtime table-tennis sessions in office and a dinner in Salem to a painting in Berlin . . .

Some of the lessons are from stories that have been written about in the past, but many of us haven't heard them. Like how a mental model can help us make peace with our world—and not think that the fruit vendor who gave us eleven bananas instead of twelve is a cheat. Lessons from a legendary football coach in America about how small things matter. And a lesson in building a sense of collective responsibility in a team from a legendary captain in Indian cricket. You will see what a former speaker in the US House of Representatives can teach us about focusing on our higher purpose and doing what we were meant to do.

In this collection of stories, you will find advice on making better decisions, thinking clearly and influencing other people. Advice on how to be a better leader and how to be a part of a great team. Lessons on navigating change, getting better and leading a life of purpose and significance. Hopefully, by the time you finish reading the book, you will find a story or two that will make you pause, reflect and do things differently.

These are stories that can help you become better.

Because the truth is, we can all get better.

We can become better professionals, better leaders and better human beings.

We can make better decisions at work and in our lives. Think better. Do better.

We can become better team players. And build great teams too. We can become the kind of people others want to be and work with.

And we can become happier too.

There's plenty of advice and wisdom out there, stuff we don't all get to hear. It never makes it to the curricula in schools and colleges. And yet, these are lessons we must all learn. Lessons we wish someone had taught us early in life.

What follows, then, are some of the lessons I have learnt about what it takes for each of us to get better, and become as good as we were meant to be. Lessons we don't always teach young people but which they must learn, nonetheless.

These are life lessons. Mostly from the school of life. Will all of them work for you? I don't know. Maybe they will. Maybe they won't.

But what's certain is that even if one of these ideas sticks in your head and makes you think or act differently—or even make one little change to your life—you would become a better person. A better version of your older self.

Now is as good a time as any to make that change.

Change your thinking. Adapt. Change your life. Henry Ford was right. If you only do what you have always done, you will only get what you have always got.

So, time to do it differently. Think differently. Act differently. Make a difference.

No point brooding and saying to yourself, 'How come no one told me that?' Now that you know, it's time to take charge. It's your life after all. You owe it to yourself.

The fun starts now.

LIFE LESSONS

I love conversations. With cab drivers and vegetable vendors, lift men and waiters at restaurants. I find it fascinating learning about their lives and hearing their perspectives. It's a terrific reminder that there is another world out there and another view. And being able to see things from that perspective, if only for a short while, is hugely rewarding.

I get a lot of my stories and lessons—and inspiration—from these conversations. Ordinary people sharing extraordinary wisdom. All you need to strike up a conversation is some curiosity, willingness to listen and a belief that everyone has a story to tell. And yes, you also need to leave aside any feeling you may have of being on a higher plane, or being smarter, wiser or superior. That's a no-no.

Try it. Strike up a conversation. And get ready for ***extraordinary wisdom from ordinary folks****.*

A Boat Ride to Remember

It is said that no visit to Kerala is complete without a boat ride in the backwaters. And predictably enough, if I was to pick one of my fondest memories of a holiday in Kerala, it would have to be of a ride in a canoe in the backwaters of Ashtamudi Lake, watching the sunrise. And the man who made it possible was the boatman—Vimalan. A man who plies his own little boat under the banner of Munroe Island Canoe Service. And to see what a fantastic job he is doing, you only need to look him up on Tripadvisor. Several grateful guests have been lavish in their praise. And in their ratings. With over 300 reviews, Vimalan has a near-five-star rating.

Vimalan speaks only Malayalam, but his son, Vijeesh—who is the boss of the business—speaks English. He guided us to the spot where we needed to go, to get on to the canoe. And we agreed to be there at 5 a.m. the next morning. Sharp. We set out in the darkness, drove for about half an hour and reached the appointed place. On the left side of the road, in the middle of nowhere, was Vimalan. Waiting in the dark. With a torch in his hand.

We parked the car and walked along as he led us down a narrow path through a little field, to the bank of the backwaters, where we saw the canoe waiting. We hopped on. And over the next 150 minutes or so, we had the ride of a lifetime.

Vimalan took us down little streams, past homes and under trees. The early morning dew and the chirping of the birds made it a veritable feast for the eyes and the ears. And for the soul too. Stepping on to a canoe can be a bit unnerving for a first-timer. Your mind instinctively flashes back to the physics class in high school. You start to jog your memory. And you try to recall Archimedes' principle and wonder whether that little log of wood can hold all four of you.

It was a Venice-like, picture-postcard experience. There were several low overhead bridges we passed under. And each time Vimalan would warn us and ask us to bend and mind our heads as we sailed under those bridges. Then, almost magically, the little stream merged into the huge Ashtamudi Lake. In time for us to watch a breathtaking sunrise. The rising sun seemed to be painting the waters of the lake in shades of red, orange and yellow. And through it all, Vimalan regaled us with non-stop banter about his myriad guests. Part boatman, part magician. And part storyteller. Vimalan made sure we all had a spectacular, memorable experience.

But it didn't end there.

As I went through the day, images from that ride kept flashing in my mind. And Vimalan's voice and our conversations with him kept playing back. That was when it dawned on me. Not only had Vimalan given us a ride to remember, he had also shared with us several life lessons.

Here, then, are some life lessons from Vimalan and that sunrise ride in a canoe:

1. *In choosing a road to take in life, don't take the easier path. Choose the one that takes you to your goals.*

We were four of us in the canoe. And Vimalan was the one doing all the hard work, navigating the canoe with an oar in his hand. We felt guilty about the hard work we were putting him through.

The little streams we were traversing merged and split. And we often wondered how Vimalan remembered which turn to take. Sometimes the current seemed to help us, while at other times it seemed against us. Once, at a fork in the water, we saw him turn into a little stream where the current was against us. Someone asked him why he did not take the other stream. The current would have been in our favour there, and that would have made it so much easier for him.

And that was when Vimalan shared with us a terrific life lesson. He said that the course he takes isn't determined by which is the easier path. It is determined by where we want to go. We needed to watch the sunrise, so he had to take us to the place from where we could see it. Taking the path where the current was on our side might have made for an easier rowing experience, but we wouldn't have been able to see the sunrise.

Now that's a lesson we would all do well to remember. Don't do what's convenient. Do what's necessary. In making a choice about which road to take, don't take the nicer, easier road. Instead, choose the road that will take you towards your goal.

2. *No matter how powerful you are, when someone says lower your head, you better do that.*

Every once in a while, we would pass under a bridge. And as we got closer, Vimalan would tell us to be careful and bend our heads. After we had done this several times, Vimalan talked about the people he had ferried on his boat. There were several VIPs in that long list. Heads of state and movie stars. Bureaucrats and business czars. And sports stars, too. He then said something which seems so profound in hindsight. He said it did not matter how high and mighty the guest on his boat was. They all had to lower their heads and bend when he asked them to.

A good reminder that in our lives and our work, we all need to let go of our egos and learn to bend, when we need to. Failing to do so can cause a lot of harm. Look around at the people you admire. Most of the time, you will find in them a sense of humility and an absence of ego. When faced with a challenge—or a bridge—everyone gets down to doing what's necessary. You may be the CEO of a billion-dollar enterprise, but on the boat, the boatman is the boss, and you need to listen to him. When he says bend, you bend. Or else.

3. *To do something special, you need to be willing to take a risk*

Somewhere along the ride, one of my friends looked at the canoe we were riding in and asked Vimalan a question: 'Where are the life jackets? Don't you have life jackets here?'

Vimalan replied that on his canoe there were no life jackets. There was just him. And then, in the reassuring voice of a man who had seen life, he shared another pearl of wisdom. In life, if you want to see magical sunrises, you need to be willing to forgo the life jacket and trust the boatman.

That's so true. In life and in business too. There isn't always a safety net. If you want to do something special, you have got to be willing to take the risk. And you have got to be willing to trust a colleague—or a partner or a friend—and believe that you are in safe hands. As someone once said, a ship is safest when it's in the harbour. But then, that's not where ships are meant to be.

Take a chance. Don't worry about failure. Trust people. And chances are you will end up doing things you may have never thought were possible. Like seeing a magical sunrise on Ashtamudi Lake.

So next time you are in Kerala, do plan a canoe ride with Vimalan. You will experience unparalleled calm and serenity as you sail down the backwaters, past the river into the lake. And you will see sights you would have never seen before. Listen closely, and Vimalan will make sure he imparts a few life lessons along the way too.

Thank you, Vimalan, for the ride of a lifetime. And for the life lessons.

Three lessons from the canoe ride:

1. In choosing which road to take, don't take the nicer, easier road. Choose the one that will take you towards your goal.
2. You may be the CEO of a billion-dollar enterprise, but on the boat, the boatman is the boss. You need to listen to him. When he says bend, you bend. Or else.
3. If you want to do something special, you have got to be willing to take the risk. And you have got to be willing to trust a colleague—or a partner or a friend—and believe that you are in safe hands.

We often think happiness lies in getting the things we want. But maybe there's an important rider to that. It starts with knowing what you want.

If you don't know ***what makes you happy****, and if you don't know what you really, really want, happiness can become a tricky thing. You can end up wanting what everyone else wants.*

And why do you want it? Only because everyone else seems to want it. And when you get it, you don't feel any happiness. Just a funny, uneasy feeling of 'what was all the fuss about?'

Knowing what you want sets you on the path to achieving true happiness.

Left or Right?

Memories. Warm and wonderful memories.

We can all recall in vivid detail a little incident from many, many years ago. And it never fails to bring a smile to our face. One of my favourite stories—from the time when my kids were, well, kids—is set in Dubai. A long time ago.

The twins—Abhishek and Shruti (or Abby and Tuts)—were about four years old. They had just started school. And since we had these long afternoon breaks at work—with offices closed between 1 p.m. and 4 p.m. in those days—it was my job to pick them up from school and take them home for lunch. It was a task I felt good about and looked forward to. Listening to the kids talk about what Miss Koita said, and what Sahil did in class, and who didn't eat the snack Mom had packed, was always a lot of fun.

And then, one day, as I walked with the kids from the school gate towards the car, Tuts said, 'I am going to sit on the right.'

'But I want to sit on the right,' said her four-minute-younger twin brother, almost immediately.

It was the rule that both kids would sit in the back, and I didn't think it mattered to any of us who sat on which side. It struck me, though, that Tuts liked to sit on the right because she would then be diagonally across from my seat, and could see me and talk to me more easily. I think she just needed to feel reassured that her dad was around. Abby, on the other hand, loved to look out of the window. He wanted to see the world around him. I think looking out also helped him fight the nausea he experienced in a moving car.

'I said it first, I want to sit on the right,' she said.

'Please, Dad, I want to sit on the right today,' said Abby.

I looked at Tuts and said, 'Let Abby sit on the right side today. And tomorrow will be your turn.' And she, the only-slightly-older-but-responsible big sister, agreed. Abby was visibly delighted. We were now almost at the car. And then Abby spoke up.

'Which is the right side?' he asked.

Ah, kids!

It is one of those kiddy conversations that still brings a smile. And as I think about it, I sometimes feel that there's a little Abby inside many, many grown-up folks. We want things because other people want them. We have no idea what those things mean, or what we will do with them once we get them. But we don't want to miss out. If it's something other people are clamouring for, we must have it too. Noticed the streak? We don't want to let other people have their way. For no reason at all.

FOMO might be a new-age acronym to describe the 'Fear of Missing Out', but the fear itself is an old one. It has been lurking around us for a long time.

Next time you find yourself wanting something that someone else wants, maybe you should hear the voice inside you asking, 'Which is the right side?'

If you can't answer that, you should know it doesn't matter to you. It's time to let other people make their little wishes come true.

> We want things because other people want them. We have no idea what those things mean, or what we will do with them once we get them, but we don't want to miss out. If it's something other people are clamouring for, we must have it too. Next time you find yourself wanting something that someone else wants, maybe you should hear the voice inside you asking, 'Which is the right side?' And let it go.

Before you start a journey, you need to know where you want to go.

That's true for the journey of life too. You need to know where you want to go.

What are you looking for in life?

And even as you try and answer that question, a good thing to remember: Success may not guarantee happiness. But there's a good chance happiness will feel like success.

Forget the destination. ***Enjoy the ride.***

In Search of the Tiger

'Welcome to the tiger capital of India.' That was what the billboards in the arrival area of Nagpur airport proclaimed. And as we read the message after getting off the plane in Nagpur, for a moment I wondered: How did they know we were here for a tiger safari?

We picked up our bags and drove off to the Kanha Tiger Reserve, in search of the tiger. We had lined up a safari for each day that we were to be there, quite like a punter who buys multiple lottery tickets to improve his odds of winning!

Early next morning, we braved the cold, jumped into the open jeep and made our way into the forest. For us city-dwellers, breathing the clean, crisp air was in itself a delightful way to start the day. We saw the sun dancing through the trees. Seeing so many birds and animals in their natural habitat was an amazing experience. We saw peacocks and deer at close quarters, including the rare barasingha.

As we crossed a pond, the driver switched off the engine. Our guide informed us—in a secretive whisper—that a tiger had been spotted here yesterday. Fear and expectation were visible on our faces. But the tiger was nowhere to be seen. Damn, wish we had been here yesterday, we felt, as we headed back. The four-hour safari was coming to an end. The disappointment was palpable. We hadn't seen a tiger.

Next morning, we set off again alongside over a hundred other jeeps, all packed with people from around the world. All with one mission. To see a tiger. And once again, the sights were pretty, no doubt. We saw jackals and wild boars to add to our list of sightings. At one place we saw pugmarks that our guide told us were of a tiger. Wow, tiger pugmarks! But we didn't see the tiger. Alas.

On day three, our safari was in the afternoon. We hoped a change in timing would bring a change in luck too. We heard a call from a bird, which the guide deciphered to mean a tiger was somewhere nearby. We waited. And waited. But it was not to be. Another safari ended with lots of sightings—but no tiger sighted.

Over our last meal at the hotel that night, we were thinking how unlucky we were. Three days. Three Safaris. And no tiger sighted. We had seen pugmarks. Heard a call. But didn't see a tiger. And then a friend said, 'Maybe we should look at it differently. We have had a great time together. We've seen some amazing animals and birds—and some terrific, picture-postcard scenery. Let's feel good about that—rather than worry about the tiger we missed.' And suddenly, the mood lifted. The food tasted better. The wine too.

Great advice, I thought. For a jungle safari, as well as for life. The problem for many of us is that we get too caught up in wanting to see the tiger, and miss out on the joy of seeing several other animals and experiencing nature at close quarters. Maybe it's time we recalibrated our goals, learnt to celebrate small wins and learnt to enjoy the ride.

The tiger is like that big prize in life that we come close to winning—but don't. It's the prize that someone else—always someone else—seems to win. Wanting to be No. 1, wanting to build a unicorn, wanting to become a billionaire, the list of 'tiger goals' is endless. Good to remember that what we are all looking for in life is happiness. Not tigers. You might think that finding the elusive tiger will make you happy. But remember, there are other routes to happiness too. Finding tigers is not always in our control. Finding happiness usually is.

Life is not so much about the destination as it is about the journey. It's the journey that makes life worth living. Simple things and little joys. That's what life is all about. Enjoy the journey. Savour the company of friends. And the sunrise. And that hot cup of tea. And nature. The tiger can wait.

Good to remember that what we are all looking for in life is happiness. Not tigers. You might think that finding the elusive tiger will make you happy. But remember, there are other routes to happiness too. Finding tigers is not always in our control. Finding happiness usually is.

Everyone plans to change and get better. Everyone dreams of a better future. We all have our ideas about what we need to do to succeed. And yet, success seems elusive. How come?

What separates the winners form the rest? It is their bias for action. The willingness to act. They don't just think about it. They do it. They have a bias for action.

Become that kind of person. ***Get that bias for action.***

Just do it.

The Monkey That Decided to Jump

Small acts, simple gestures can sometimes remind us of powerful lessons. Like it happened with me some years ago.

We had got back home after a week-long celebration of a wedding in the family. We reached late at night and, as you might expect, we were tired. When we woke up—rather late—the next morning, guess what we found? A nice, hot breakfast that had been sent to our home by a kind, old friend in our apartment complex. The maid wasn't back at work, the refrigerator was bare and we weren't up to making our own breakfast. So you can understand our sense of delight and gratitude at this wonderful gesture from a friend. She made our day.

But that wasn't all. She also got me thinking. We usually have the right idea but don't always end up acting on it. How come we miss out on opportunities to create delight for other people in our lives? This was a lovely gesture from a friend. And I wished I had done that more often for others too. I am sure if the friend had called and asked if we needed help (like many of us thoughtfully do), we'd have said no thanks. But she didn't ask. She sent the food over. And that made all the difference.

Saying 'Let me know how I can help' is the equivalent of telling someone 'We must catch up'. It's hollow, empty. And the truth is, you both realize this.

I thought of the many times I might have offered to help a friend—and how each time they had declined. I thought of how we make an offer to help but don't do anything. Because very few people actually respond with a specific request for help. As a result, we miss out on an opportunity to help others. We ask other people 'How can I help?' when in fact we should be asking ourselves that question. And then doing something about it. It's ever so rare that we proactively do something to help! Maybe we all should.

The friend's gesture reminded me of an old quiz question: There are three little monkeys sitting on a tree, above a pond. One of those monkeys decides to jump into the pond. How many monkeys left on the tree? Come on, take a guess.

Two, did you say? Or was your response 'zero', since you figured that if one monkey jumps, the others too would follow? Or did you say three?

If your answer was three, congratulations. You are right. The monkey only decided to jump. It didn't *actually* jump. Aren't we all a bit like that?

We plan. We decide. We think. But we don't take action. Have you decided to lose weight? Yes? And you are wondering why you haven't lost weight, although you had decided three months ago? Success in life comes not from deciding to do things—but from doing them. Results are born of action, not intent. The Nike guys were right. 'Just do it,' they said. We could all benefit by building a strong bias for action. Become someone who doesn't think about it or talk about it—but someone who does it.

So next time you want to help friends who've come back after a long and tiring trip, don't ask if you can help. If you've been thinking of calling that old aunt you haven't spoken to in years, stop thinking about it. If you've been meaning to help that friend who is looking for a job, do something about it. Today. Don't ask, 'How can I help?' Or, 'Let me know if I can help.' Chances are most people won't come back and bother you for help. So next time, don't ask. Do something about it.

Take that first step. Don't just think about it. Do it. Now!

Don't ask other people 'How can I help?' Ask yourself that question. And then do something about it. It's ever so rare that we proactively do something to help! Maybe we all should.

Get that bias for action. Don't just think about it. Do it.

GETTING BETTER

When was the last time someone told you about something you do wrong? Not about a blunder—but something about the way you behave, or the way you speak, or the way you do things?

And more importantly, is there someone in your life whom you can count on—to help point out those little flaws and help you set it right?

People who get it right in life are constantly working to get better. And they have someone helping them get better. You should too.

Find someone who helps you make those minor adjustments that can make you unstoppable. A person who helps you adapt to change. Someone who reminds you that the old version of yourself is getting outdated and becoming a misfit in a changing world.

Get a 'Let's make it right' partner.

The Alteration Tailor

Looking good never goes out of fashion. Which is why you find articles on style and trends not only in fashion magazines but in business journals too. I remember reading a column where a style guru talked about her 'Five tips to help you look your very best'. One tip on that stylist's list caught my attention. It was this: Get yourself an alteration tailor.

Rather unusual advice, I thought. And the more I thought about it, the more sense it seemed to make. And it made me wonder: How many of us have an alteration tailor? Do you have one?

The stylist's logic was simple. You can buy expensive new clothes. You can fill your wardrobe with trendy fashion statements. But for them to look good on you, you often need to make minor alterations. Like adjusting that length a bit. Or loosening it up a little near the waist. Teeny-weeny changes that can make a big difference. An alteration tailor can help turn 'looking good' into 'looking great'.

As I thought about all that an alteration tailor can do for us, it struck me that this was great advice. Not only from a style perspective, but for our lives too. An alteration tailor can help us look good and be the best we can be. What we need in life, then, are two alteration tailors. One for our clothes, and another for our lives. We need a friend, partner, mentor or coach—who does for our lives what an alteration tailor would do for our clothes.

We need someone who can point out those little adjustments we need to make to get better, and can help us make those changes that allow us to become the best version of ourselves. Because at the end of the day, looking good is not about having fancy brands or large wardrobes. It's about having comfortable, well-fitting clothes that make us feel good. And being a good leader is not about having an MBA or being the alumnus of a prestigious school. It's about playing to your strengths and being a good human being. The alteration tailor can be a powerful ally in your life's journey. Here's how.

An alteration tailor prepares you for change. We change, our worlds change. What worked yesterday may not work today. That newly acquired extra flab around the waist might mean that you need to loosen up the shirt a bit. Just promoted to be a team leader? It might mean allowing your people to make mistakes and learn—and not doing their jobs for them. An alteration tailor helps ensure you are not force-fitting outdated models. The reassuring presence of an alteration tailor on your side can help you embrace change.

An alteration tailor also tells us the value of paying attention to detail, and making sure you get it right. That's a terrific leadership trait. You might have a well-fitting blazer, but if one of those buttons on the cuff is missing, it won't feel right wearing it. That little flaw, that missing button, needs fixing. It's not about whether anyone else will even notice the missing button. You will. An alteration tailor can help fix that.

We all have new, unused clothes in our wardrobes. Something that we picked up in a moment of temptation, only to discover it didn't fit too well. The alteration tailor helps you to make the most of what you already have. Instead of letting it lie there, he makes it wearable. So you don't need to worry about adding to your wardrobe. That unused shirt is a good metaphor for our lives. We've got all it takes to succeed. We have unused strengths. We need to learn to use them. What we need is someone who can tweak our traits a little and tell us where we are going wrong. And help us get it right.

Don't worry about acquiring new skills. Focus instead on putting your strengths to better, fuller use. You don't need one more qualification. Or one more Ivy League training programme. What you need is someone who points to, say, your short temper and helps you fix it. Or nudges you to let go of your diffidence and become more assertive. Or reminds you to look for and appreciate the good in other people, helping you become a better team player. Small alterations, which can potentially lead to big impact.

The alteration tailor can also help us discover the keys to better relationships, to more enduring relationships. A difference of opinion does not have to mean the end of a friendship. A temporary performance issue at work does not mean you need to change jobs. An alteration tailor helps ensure you don't throw away a pair of trousers just because a button has gone missing. Minor hiccups can be, and must be, fixed.

Many of us complain that there are no alteration tailors. We seldom hear about them. Truth is, they exist. They are just a bit harder to find. Look for them, and you are certain to find one. Usually, very close to you. You only need to look. Seek and you shall find.

Do yourself a favour. Go find yourself two alteration tailors today. One for your clothes, and one for your life. You deserve it.

Become the best you can be.

An alteration tailor can help us look good and be the best we can be. What we need in life, then, are two alteration tailors. One for our clothes, and another for our lives. We need a friend, partner, mentor or coach—who does for our lives what an alteration tailor would do for our clothes. We need someone who can point out those little adjustments we need to make to get better. And help us make those changes that allow us to become the best version of ourselves.

Everyone wants options. Backup plans and safety nets. But if you look at some of the great people who changed the world, you would often see a pattern. They had no choice, no option, but to make a success of whatever it was they were working on.

Get that mindset. Failure is not an option.

If you want to make sure you don't give up on your dreams and aspirations, here's what you should do: Make sure you understand that ***giving up is not an option****. You have no choice but to persevere.*

Having No Option Is the Best Option

It's a daily ritual. Well, almost. Every morning at 6 a.m., my wife and I step out for a walk. The intent is to walk for an hour and get our day's quota of physical activity. It also allows us to catch up on conversation. As we step out of our home, we have a choice of two alternative routes we can take for the hour-long walk.

The first option—let's call it 'the long road'—is to take a circuitous 6 km walk around the area we live in. It's a path that circumnavigates the entire neighbourhood: a round that is along the perimeter of the area. We go past an assortment of villas, apartments, then around office buildings. Then we reach the local shopping complex, and go past a temple and a school. Finally, we find ourselves on the road back home after completing one long loop. A full sixty-minute walk.

The other option—let's call it 'round and round'—is to walk from home to a circular garden about six minutes away. We do four rounds of the garden, each of which takes about twelve minutes. And then walk back home along the same path, completing the hour-long morning ritual.

Both the routes have their own charms. But I've noticed something interesting about the two choices. On days when we take the long road, we get engrossed in conversation. We don't think too much about the walk itself, or the time or the distance. Once we decide to take that long road, we know that it will be an hour before we are back home. There's no other way out.

But when we take the option of doing four rounds of the garden, something strange seems to happen. Some days, after completing the first round, one of us would feel a slight tightening of the calf muscle. On other days, after the second round, I would sense the aroma of the home-made filter coffee beckoning. I can't wait to go home! Sometimes, as we complete round two, the wife would say, 'I am feeling tired today.' 'Ah, you didn't sleep too well last night, did you?' I would ask, and then look into her eyes and at the road that would take us back home. Often, after the third round, I would be convinced that it was in fact round four we completed—and not round three. So, time to head back. You get the drift, right?

Result? On most days when we take the round-and-round option, we actually end up walking for less than an hour. When we set off from home, our intent is always the same: walk for an hour. But the presence of an option to walk less than an hour actually results in outcomes that are different. We take the soft option.

And that set me thinking. Does this happen to us in other walks of life too? The existence of an option, an alternative, often makes us deviate from our chosen path, leading to suboptimal outcomes. Success comes through grit, through sticking it out. And through staying the course even when the going gets tough. Giving up is easy. And when you have an option, it gets easier.

Businesses and leaders love having a Plan B. Maybe we all need to rethink that.

Plan B is meant to be an alternative that you can resort to when the preferred path, Plan A, is coming apart. Failing. Plan B is not meant to be an option simply because Plan A is proving to be a tough, long haul. But that's the trap we fall into. We are quick to abandon the long road to the big prize in favour of a short cut that doesn't quite get us the same rewards. The consequence? We give up. Too soon. At the first hint of trouble, we abandon our stated objective. Forget the first hint of trouble—we imagine there's trouble. It's almost as if we start seeking out the negatives and the downsides when there's a tempting Plan B in sight! Choice, then, isn't always a good thing. Sometimes not having any other option can be the fuel that powers you along the long road to success.

Reminds me of something that happened several years ago, in the third century BCE. General Xiang Yu sent some troops across the Yangtze River in China, to fight the Qin dynasty. Once they landed across the river, General Yu ordered the ships to be set ablaze. He then told his soldiers the hard truth: 'You have a choice, young men. Either you fight and win the war, or you die.'

Might be good idea for you to consider too. Burn your ships once the soldiers land. Shut out Plan B. In business and in life, we cling on to our escape routes, our Plan Bs. Because we value the safety of retreat. We want to avoid the risks of progress. And we give up on the challenge that precedes any achievement.

Next time, take the long road. Burn the ships. Have a plan B? Junk it. You'll discover new ways—and new passion and resolve—to make Plan A work.

> Success comes through grit, through sticking it out. And through staying the course even when the going gets tough. Giving up is easy. And when you have an option, it gets easier. Junk Plan B. Sometimes not having any other option can be the fuel that powers you along the long road to success.

Sport is a terrific metaphor for life. And sport reveals character like nothing else can. Which is why I think it is a good idea to have teams at work play some sport.

Sport can also teach us many, many life lessons.

They say the only ball that matters in cricket is the next one. It doesn't matter whether you had hit a six off the previous ball or were beaten neck and crop. The past is irrelevant. It's the next ball that counts.

They say that in golf too: the only shot that matters is the next one. And in tennis: the next point is the one you need to win.

If you think about it, life is like that too. Don't worry about the past. Even if you've failed, it's the next chance that matters. Make it count. And even if you've been successful in the past, don't take it for granted. Tomorrow is another day. You start afresh.

Make it count. ***Sport is life.*** *Play the game.*

What Table Tennis Can Teach Us about Life

Do you have a table-tennis table in the workplace? A TT table was the common feature in several of the offices I worked in. I would look forward to lunch hour every day. Not for the food or the lunch-hour conversations, but for the post-lunch TT game!

Apart from being a stressbuster, it was also a great leveller. After all, where else would you find the rookie accounts officer hammering the CFO? As I sat back and thought of the fun and games, I couldn't help thinking of the life and leadership lessons that the daily ping-pong sessions threw up.

Here, then, are five lessons from the ping-pong table.

1. Not too high, not too low

Table tennis is a simple game after all. Hit the ball—not so low that it doesn't clear the net, and not so high that it doesn't land on the table. Most things in business—and in life—are like that. It's about finding balance. You can't be so hard on your people that no one wants to work with you—and you can't be so soft that no one takes you seriously. You can't be too adventurous. Nor too conservative. And remember, *you* have to make that adjustment. The net won't get any lower. Nor will the table become any longer.

2. The two best players don't always make the strongest team

We often think great teams are about having talented individual players, the superstars. But in those games of table tennis, we learnt how the two best players didn't always end up winning as a team. Teamwork is about learning to get the best out of your team-mate, covering for the other's weaknesses and helping him (or her) play to their full potential.

3. Small things matter

The TT table cost quite a bit. We had some expensive racquets too. And yet, there were days when we couldn't play—because we had run out of table-tennis balls! A ball only cost some Rs 15, but without it life would come to a standstill. And we seemed to worry about the ball only when it wasn't there. Good question to ask yourself: What are the ping-pong balls in your life? Who are those almost forgotten, seemingly insignificant folks without whom your life wouldn't be the same?

4. Blame it on the racquet

It happened all the time. Someone would hit a bad shot or lose a few points—and then what would he do? Look disgustedly at his racquet and reach out for a change of racquets. It was almost as if they were saying: 'The problem is not with me, it's that damn racquet!' When things go wrong, we always look for someone else to blame. A bad workman—even in sport—still blames his tools. The racquet is only as good as the person holding it. Good lesson to remember.

5. The only point that matters is the next one

Never mind what the score in the game is, all you have to do is win the next point. And the next. That's a good attitude to have in life. Don't worry about the last point. That's history. Over. Finished. Focus on the next point. No matter how strong the opposition, back yourself to win the next point. And the next. The next point, the next ball, the next shot. That's all that matters. That's what sport is all about. Heck, isn't that what life is all about?

Five lessons from the ping-pong table:

1. Don't hit the ball too high or too low. Remember, you have to make the adjustment.
2. The two best players don't always make the strongest team.
3. Small things matter.
4. A bad workman blames his tools.
5. The only point that matters is the next one. In sport. And in life.

There's an old saying. Life is like riding a bicycle. If you want to keep your balance, you need to keep moving.

That is so true, even today. ***Standing still is never an option****, and if you do so, a fall is almost guaranteed. But the euphoria of riding the bike can make us believe we are infallible.*

And that's when the trouble begins.

Time to Get Your Own Shot Clock!

It was the 1950s. The sport of basketball was in trouble. Games were beginning to drag. Excitement was dwindling, and the crowds were staying away. Wondering why?

Well, here's what would happen. Once a team got a lead in the game, they would deliberately slow down the game. They would try and hold on to the ball for as long as they could. The team in the lead would pass the ball from one team-mate to another, depriving the opponents of a chance to catch up. They wouldn't bother with shooting and scoring points. So much so that in one NBA game, the scoreline at the end read 19–18. Sounds unbelievable today, doesn't it?

And then, in 1954, came an innovation that transformed basketball. The shot clock. Danny Biasone is the man credited with its introduction. He is the man credited with changing the face of basketball. He introduced the clock—a countdown timer—and a new rule came into force. Once a team got possession of the ball, they had twenty-four seconds in which to take a shot at the basket. If they failed to do that, the ball would pass over to the opposing team. Result? Both teams now had no option but to try and score points throughout the game. There was never a dull moment, and often the winner was decided only in the dying moments of the game. The impact was dramatic. The pace of the game picked up. Average points per game went up from 79 to 107. And attendance, too, went up by 40 per cent.

Basketball's shot clock has got the authorities in other sports thinking too. Tennis officials are experimenting with a shot clock, no doubt aimed at putting an end to the endless ball-bouncing we see before every serve. And underwear-adjusting too. Golf is toying with the idea as well, to try and speed up the game, and get golfers to take a shot without a million practice swings.

But it strikes me that more than tennis players and golf pros, it's you and I who need to get our own shot clocks. And yes, every organization, every business needs one too.

We see several businesses do what the team in the lead in basketball used to do. They build a large, profitable enterprise—and a dominant share—and then sit back and rest on their laurels. They don't innovate. They don't feel the need to do anything new. And they die. Take Kodak, for instance. A shot clock could have reminded Kodak that they needed to change. That if they didn't move forward, they risked losing their customers and their entire camera film business. A clock like that would have goaded Kodak to go digital and saved them from bankruptcy.

As individuals, we are sometimes guilty of falling into the same trap. We work hard. We deliver. We get elevated to a position we had always wanted. And then we take our foot off the pedal and move into cruise-control mode. We think no one will notice. But our teams pick up that change. The organization's performance reflects the slackening-up. And business begins to go south. We could all do with a shot clock that would remind us that sitting pretty on past successes is not an option. We need to make progress, grow and learn in order to stay relevant. And if we don't do that, we risk losing what we have so carefully built up.

And I am sure we all need that shot clock in our personal lives too. To remind us to spend time with the family. Go out on that dinner date with the spouse. Be there with the children. We all need reassurance. Constant reassurance. A countdown timer that says, 'You'd better do this again quickly—or else!' would work wonders, I am sure. Use the shot clock to guide yourself in your personal life and watch the quality of your relationships improve.

Time, then, to get your own little shot clock. Before it's too late.

> We could all do with a shot clock that would remind us that sitting pretty on past successes is not an option. We need to make progress, grow and learn in order to stay relevant. And if we don't do that, we risk losing what we have so carefully built up. Taking your foot off the pedal is not an option.

Style versus substance is an oft-mentioned debate. And it's no surprise that everyone agrees that substance is what matters, that it's the real deal. But the mistake we make, even as we argue and win the debate, is that we dismiss style as irrelevant and completely useless. That is a terrible mistake. A mistake we often make in resolving such debates. In trying to prove that one thing is better than the other, we try and prove that the other thing is useless and inconsequential, when all we had to do was to show that it mattered less. Soft skills versus hard skills, skill versus attitude, experience versus potential, the list is endless. A good thing to remember: ***We are not as rational as we think.***

Even as you are convinced about what matters more, pause and think about how the less important bit might still matter. Do that, and you will be surprised.

Judge a Book by Its Cover, Everyone Does!

Chia-Jung Tsay is an associate professor at the University College London School of Management. She is also the kind of multitalented person we all admire. She has a PhD in organizational behaviour and psychology, and another PhD in music from Harvard. She is an accomplished pianist, too, having performed at Carnegie Hall. As she watched one of those talent contests on TV one night, a question popped up in her head. How do people judge performances in a music contest? The psychologist-cum-pianist was keen to find an answer.

She got over 1000 people to participate in a study that aimed to find some answers to that question. The participants ranged from novice musicians to professional music adjudicators. In the experiment, they were handed out clips from an international piano competition. They were then asked to rate the performances and guess who the winner of the competition was. And here's the interesting bit.

The participants were divided into three groups. One group was given audio clips—they could only hear the pianists and not see them. The second group of people was shown video clips, with the audio on mute—so they could see the performers but not hear them play the piano. And the third group was shown video clips with the audio intact—so they could both watch and hear the pianists. Based on what they had heard, or seen, or heard and seen—the participants had to guess who had won the competition.

Now everyone will tell you that in a music competition, it is the sound that matters the most. But guess what? In Dr Tsay's experiment, the participants who watched the silent videos did the best. Think about that. Incredibly, the group that couldn't hear the music at all was able to identify the winners, better than the group that could only hear the music. Participants who saw and heard the pianists did a lot worse than those who could only see the pianists.

The message from the study was clear. We depend more on visual cues when making judgements—even about musical performances. It turns out, musical performances are more than just about the sounds musicians make! Piano teachers focus on teaching kids how to get their pianos to produce the best sounds. But competition judges seem to be looking at something else when it comes to picking the winners.

A variant of the piano experiment plays out in many areas of our lives. Like recruitment, for instance. In a typical job interview, we are looking for ability, as well as intellect and experience. But we get swayed by the looks of the candidate, more than we'd like to acknowledge. As Dr Tsay says, 'We must be more mindful of our inclination to depend on visual information. At the expense of the content that we actually value as more relevant to our decisions.'

Sure, we need to watch out for the trap. Don't allow visual cues to dominate our decision-making, even when it is irrelevant. We also need to recognize the role of visual communication and optics—they impact our judgement far more than we think. And other people's judgements too. It's good to be a proficient pianist. But it's even better to look like one!

At work, we sometimes worry about not being recognized, despite doing the hard work and delivering great results. Yet apart from doing a good job, we need to focus on 'being seen' to be doing a good job too. Former Australian cricketer Ian Chappell talks about some fabulous advice his father gave him: 'If you want to be a cricketer, son, start by looking like one.' That's great leadership advice too. If you want to be a leader, start by looking like one. If you want to be a winner, start by looking like one.

And that's true for teams and organizations as well. Think of the huddle that the Indian cricket team engages in. Everyone agrees it smells like team spirit. Watch how they celebrate. Notice how we watch intently when TV cameras capture the scenes in the dressing room. We look for clues. We look at who the captain is speaking with, what are the expressions on the players' faces. All these go into our judgement of how good the team is!

Reminds me of my early days at Unilever in India (the good old HLL). All the directors of the company would wear ties to work. The rest of us never wore a tie. Except one high-performing general manager, who very soon went on to get promoted and became one of the youngest directors at HLL.

This is not a suggestion to say you should fake it till you make it. Just a reminder that ability matters, and talent rules, sure. But combine that with appearance and 'looking the part'. And you help yourself, increasing the odds that you would succeed.

'Don't judge a book by its cover' is advice we've all heard. But we haven't heeded it, have we? We get attracted by the cover and instinctively reach out for that book at the airport bookstore. Publishers recognize the huge role that a book cover plays in ensuring the success of the book. Of course, a good cover won't ensure a bad book's success. You need to write a good book. But having done that, you shouldn't stop. Get a great cover. Make sure you look good.

Which is also why executive presence is so important, and yet so underrated. How do you come across to other people? Do you inspire trust and confidence? Do you look like someone people want to work with? Leadership development often focuses on helping people get better. Time to focus on helping them look better too. How you speak, how you dress, your mannerisms, the gravitas you display, all these matter, far more than they are given credit for. Next time you are meeting customers or interacting with your team, think of the piano contest. Imagine that your video is on mute and you are being judged!

In our time-starved world, people don't have the patience to dig deep. They don't have time to discover what's beneath the surface. A good book cover, the looks and the appearance, these serve as filters. Hacks that enable you to discover a real gem.

Next time, try and avoid the bias of visual cues in your judgements. And even as you do that, remember, that's the way of the world.

Don't short-change yourself. Don't kid yourself into believing otherwise. It doesn't matter whether you like it or not.

Appearances matter.

> Next time, try and avoid the bias of visual cues in your judgements. And even as you do that, remember, that's the way of the world. Appearances matter.

It was G.K. Chesterton who said, 'Anything worth doing is worth doing badly.' And that is such powerful advice.

What stops us from doing our best work is the fear of doing something badly. We wait, we plan. We prepare. We dream. We do everything except actually doing it. And what we don't always recognize is that doing it badly, doing it often, making mistakes and getting it wrong, is what helps us get better, paving the way for that ultimate masterpiece. All those hours of practice eventually pay off.

If you want to write a bestseller, you could spend a lot of time looking for inspiration, thinking about the killer idea, reading up the masters, taking a course perhaps, thinking some more. Or you could write. Just write. Maybe 500 words a day.

Which do you think gives you your best chance of writing a bestseller? Think about it. Actually, no, ***don't just think about it****.*

Quantity versus Quality

The 'quantity vs quality' debate is an old one. And it came back to my mind when I read a book called *Art and Fear* by David Bayles and Ted Orland. In it, they tell an interesting story about a ceramics class, a story with a valuable lesson for us all.

On the first day of class, the teacher announced that he was dividing the class into two groups. One group, he said, would be evaluated at the end of the course on the quality of their work. And the other group would be evaluated on the quantity of work they produced.

The methodology was simple. On the final day of the programme, the teacher would bring in a weighing machine to the class. He would weigh the pots that each member of the 'quantity' group had produced. Over 30 kg of pots would get the student an A grade. Twenty kilograms and above would merit a B. And under 20 kg would mean a C.

And what about the 'quality' group? Students in this group only needed to submit one pot each for evaluation. Their best creation. If it was judged to be perfect, they would get an A. Good work could get you a B. And poor work would only merit a C.

Something interesting happened on the final day of class. It turned out that the highest-quality pots were all the handiwork of the students in the 'quantity' group. That's right. How come?

Students in this group got busy making lots and lots of pots. They made plenty of mistakes too. But they learnt from those mistakes. They got better. And all the hands-on practice meant that they managed to create some very fine good-quality pots.

Students in the 'quality' group got to work on creating that perfect pot. They kept planning and thinking and fantasizing about the masterpiece. They were obsessed with the idea of creating that one perfect pot. More obsession than action. Result? They didn't quite manage to produce work of great significance.

Interesting, isn't it? I am sure at some time or the other, we've all been in the middle of a quantity-versus-quality debate. And if you were like me, you too would have weighed in on the side of quality. We have all heard the dictum that quality matters and quantity doesn't count.

Maybe we need a rethink. It's no longer a case of quantity vs quality. Truth is, quantity leads to quality.

The obsession with quality can mean you are 'thinking' about getting it right. You plan. You prepare. You analyse. But you don't act. You are afraid you'll get it wrong. But when quantity becomes the driver, we are all quick to swing into action. We get going. We make mistakes. And we set them right. We reach a dead end sometimes. And when that happens, we retrace our steps and find another way. Through it all, we gain experience and get better, which leads to better-quality work.

If you want to bake a cake, a fabulous cake, you could scour the Net for the perfect recipe. You could ask your friends, watch YouTube videos and read up a lot of books on how to bake the perfect cake.

Or you could get into the kitchen and get to work on baking a cake. Make one that doesn't rise. And another that's a bit hard. And another and another. Chances are, you will soon make a cake that everyone will love.

And if you are a sales guy, this could work for you too. If you tilt towards the quality argument, you might choose to tap high-value clients, instead of focusing on making more calls. You spend time researching the big players in the industry. You drop the small guys. You read up on the target company. You try and find a connect. And then wait for an auspicious day to call.

Instead, you just need to get out there and make a call. Visit that small customer. Chances are, he will give you feedback or share an insight that will help you sharpen your pitch. And he will guide you to another potential customer. As you meet more of them, you actually increase the odds of winning that large customer.

So if you want to do better, you should take a lesson from that ceramics class. Focus on quantity. Do more. Get your hands dirty. Make mistakes. Don't obsess about perfection. It's okay to fail. Get started. Get busy.

And suddenly, almost magically, the masterpiece will come to life.

The obsession with quality can mean you are 'thinking' about getting it right. You plan. You prepare. You analyse. But you don't act. You are afraid you'll get it wrong. But when quantity becomes the driver, we are all quick to swing into action. We get going. We make mistakes. And we set them right. And through it all, we gain experience and get better, which leads to better-quality work.

IT'S ALL IN THE MIND

Do the right thing, and don't worry about what people will think. In any case, most people are too busy doing their own thing—they don't really have time to waste thinking about you.

Yet we worry. And we try and live our lives to someone else's script. We try and march to someone else's tune. Bad idea.

Do what you do best. **Do it your way.** *And give yourself your best chance to succeed.*

What Will People Think?

If you are a basketball fan, you've probably heard of Wilt Chamberlain.

Wilt was an all-time great NBA basketball player. Standing tall at over seven feet, he had several records to his name. He was the first player to score over 30,000 points in his career. He held the record for the highest number of points in a season. And in a historic game in March 1962, Wilt scored 100 points, becoming the first player to score 100 points in a game, an achievement that remains unmatched to date.

Wilt was a great basketball player. But there's a lesser-known aspect of his game that holds interesting lessons for us.

Despite a career average of over 30 points a game, Wilt had a problem, a chink in his armour. He was very poor with free throws. Imagine! Here was a player who could get past defenders with ridiculous ease. A player who could score points from all over the court. And yet, he would struggle to put the ball through the hoop from fifteen feet, with no defender to obstruct him.

His free throw conversion rate was 50.1 per cent. A terrible number when you consider that the average in the NBA was about 75 per cent.

So what is a free throw in basketball? When a player is 'fouled'—or unfairly obstructed from taking a shot at the basket—he gets a free throw. It's a chance to take a shot at the basket from fifteen feet, with nobody from the opposition team allowed to come in the way. Simple. Most players have a somewhat similar routine when they take a free throw. They line up at the designated spot. They hold the ball at eye level. And then, with the palm placed at shoulder height, they aim for the basket. That's what most players do.

Most players. Not Rick Barry—another all-time great. When it came to free throws, Rick had a very different technique. He preferred to hold the ball between his knees and throw it underhand. Yes, you read that right.

Underhand. Perfectly legal, but a method shunned by most big-name players. The method was derisively referred to as the 'granny style'. But for Rick, it was effective. His career free-throw percentage was a phenomenal 89.3 per cent, with a high of 94 per cent in one season. Granny style, but very, very effective.

With a free-throw percentage of under 50 per cent, Wilt was desperate to find new ways to improve that number. In the 1962 season, he decided to give Rick Barry's underhand method a try. And it worked. His free throw conversion rate improved. And it also helped him score a record-breaking 100 points in a single game.

In that famous game, he converted twenty-eight of the thirty-two free throw attempts he made. A conversion rate of 87.5 per cent. All done underhand. Granny style.

You'd have thought that after switching to the underhand technique and finding success, Wilt would have stayed with it, for the rest of his career, and improved his career conversion rate thereafter. He didn't. Next season, he went back to shooting overhead—not underhand. And his conversion rate slipped again from 61 per cent in the previous season back to about 50 per cent.

Why did he do that? Why would a great basketball player pass up a technique that improved his game? Hear it from Wilt.

'I felt silly,' said Wilt. 'I felt like a sissy!'

He must have wondered, 'What will people think?' And because he felt that way, he went back to a better-looking—but less effective—technique.

Many of us fall into this trap. We put 'looking good' ahead of 'being effective'. We care too much about how it looks, or about what people will say. And in the process, we compromise our effectiveness. Our own greatness.

Being aware of the Chamberlain way can make a difference. For individuals as well as for businesses.

I am reminded of the breakfast buffet at my favourite hotel chain. Like most hotels, they too offered a wide assortment of teas to choose from. There were exotic teas, hand-picked from around the world. You were spoilt for choice, as you would be in most of the better hotels. But did all those expensive teas make for a great tea-drinking experience? Not quite.

And then the hotel came up with an idea. They started offering readymade tea, the way it is served on the streets of India, in cheap-looking, 'cutting chai' glasses. With milk and sugar. And ginger and cardamom too. It was an instant hit. Suddenly everyone wanted it. They even had a man, dressed as a roadside vendor, go around the coffee shop on his bicycle. And he was very soon the most popular guy at the breakfast buffet. You couldn't help thinking: How come no other hotel thought of this before? It was not that the hotels did not know that Indians love their tea this way. But something was holding the hotels back. How could a five-star hotel serve the kind of tea that you could find at any roadside stall? Wouldn't look good, would it? What about our brand image? It was too downmarket for a five-star hotel, no? And then, one hotel decided to try it. And by God, it worked! Cutting chai is now a regular feature in many five-star hotels.

Good lesson to remember. Some of the best ideas are sometimes not so sexy, not so cool. It's tempting for us to prioritize what 'looks good' over what 'works well'. We worry about what people will say, what they will think. And we end up choosing the suboptimal option.

Are you sometimes guilty of doing that too? Are you compromising your effectiveness—only to look good or to please people? Think about it. Don't let that happen to you.

Feeling like a sissy may not be such a bad thing after all.

We put 'looking good' ahead of 'being effective'. We care too much about how it looks, or about what people will say. And in the process, we compromise our effectiveness. Our own greatness.

Self-belief is big. Leaders have a lot of it. No matter how daunting the challenge, they back themselves to get it right. To win. But there can be a downside too.

That sense of wanting to be all-powerful can sometimes make them feel that they are the ones who make the world go round. That everything that is happening is due to their actions. And sometimes leaders make the mistake of finding causal relationships between actions and outcomes—even when there is really no connection. Blame it on insecurity perhaps. Or the need for control. And the need to garner credit and let the world know 'I did it'. Or, 'It happened because of me.'

Good leaders don't do that. They know there is a wide world out there—and it is colleagues and partners and processes that help make things happen.

Recognize that not all outcomes are due to your actions. *And in some cases, they may have nothing to do with you.*

Humbling thought, no?

The Man Who Kept the Giraffes Away

In his delightful little book *The Art of Thinking Clearly,* Rolf Dobelli tells an interesting story. It's a story that provides a fascinating insight into leadership behaviour and could hold a lesson for all of us.

The story goes that every morning in a little town, a man in a yellow shirt and a red hat would come to a busy traffic junction. Just before nine o'clock, he would wave his hat around wildly. And after ten minutes of frantic waving, he would disappear.

One day, a policeman went up to him and asked: 'What are you doing here?'

'I am keeping the giraffes away!' said the man.

'But there aren't any giraffes here,' said the cop.

'See, I am doing such a good job!' said the man.

The story might bring a smile to your face. And if you think about it, you might even be able to relate it to what we see our leaders doing! Leaders like to believe they are in control and are making things happen. Leaders are quick to attribute outcomes to their own actions—even when there may be no real correlation. Seen that happening? Yes? Thought as much.

Why does that happen? How can leaders avoid this trap? Here are four simple tips to ponder.

1. Get over the illusion of control

Accept that you don't control everything. Not everything that happens around you happens because of you. No one needs you to prove that as a leader you are in control of everything. You don't have to control everything. It's okay.

2. Change, break away from tradition

You may have been doing things a certain way for many years, but if it doesn't make sense today, stop doing it. 'We have always done it this way' is not enough reason to continue doing it that way forever. Be willing to be challenged. Stop waving your favourite red hat if it's not really required.

3. Don't look for credit

Let go of the desperate need to take credit. You don't need to be able to link every success to your own effort. It does not have to be the case that the sales team is doing well because of what you said to them at the conference in Pattaya last year. Or last week. That intern who left you ten years ago and is now a CEO elsewhere—maybe it's because he is good, and not because of what you taught him while he worked with you for a year. It's not always about you.

4. You don't have to have a reason for everything

Stop searching for an associated reason for everything that happens. Accept that sometimes, things just happen. The need to attribute a cause often makes leaders look for connections between their own actions and the outcomes they are seeing. And once they find a link—however phoney—they shut out the evidence and lose sight of the real reason why something's happening. Or not happening.

As leaders, we are all guilty of spending, nay wasting, company resources waving the red hat and believing that's what is keeping the giraffes away. Next time you see a leader waving his red hat, you should do something too.

Wave a red flag. Stop it.

> Stop believing you are the one making everything happen. Get over that illusion of control. Remember, you might just be the one keeping the giraffes away at the traffic light.

Mental models are fun. They are a useful tool for understanding our minds, our world, ourselves. And just being familiar with mental models can help us live better, happier lives. They help us better understand the world we live in.

Most times we are responsible for our own misery. Which is a good thing perhaps, because once you realize that, you also realize that getting rid of the misery is in your control too. Our minds often trick us into fearing the worst, into imagining that the world is conspiring against us. But that is rarely the case. We tend to attribute motives to other people's actions. And words.

***Thinking differently can make you happier.** Happiness is a choice.*

Choose wisely.

A Razor That Changed My Life

Have you heard of Hanlon's razor? It is a mental model. A way of thinking. It will change the quality of your relationships. Ever since I learnt about it some years ago, it's made me a happier person. So I thought I must tell you about it too.

Hanlon's razor states, 'Never attribute to malice that which can be explained by negligence.' Next time you feel hard done by, don't attribute it to ill-will or evil intent. Never do that. Think of it as an aberration. Chances are it was an oversight.

Got only eleven bananas when you paid for twelve? No, the fruit vendor is not a cheat. He miscounted. Your friends went for a movie without telling you? No, it's not that no one loves you any more. They forgot. That's all.

Think about what happens when something goes wrong or when we feel hard done by. Our instinctive response is to attribute motives to other people's actions. Someone did it on purpose, to hurt us. To harm our cause. And once we let that thought into our head, we get upset, agitated. Angry with the person who did it. And we resolve to get even, to avenge that hurt. Happens, no?

When it does, remember Hanlon's razor. Never attribute to malice that which can be explained by negligence. Or stupidity. Tell yourself it was an oversight, an unintended mistake. And it is not that the person—or the world—is conspiring against you. If you think of it that way, it won't upset you.

Imagine there's an important project you have been working on. In fact, you have been leading it together with a colleague. It's going well, and you are hoping a successful project will do good things for the company. And for your career. And then you discover that your colleague has sent a mail to the boss, and to all the stakeholders, updating them on the project status. Without marking you on it. You only learn about the mail when it gets mentioned in a meeting. You feel betrayed. You are convinced your colleague did it to hog all the credit. To make the bosses think he is the one doing all the work. And to ensure he gets that promotion ahead of you. You don't want to work with such a terrible guy. You even say some nasty things about him to a friend. Those words reach his ears too in no time. And the relationship gets soured.

Think about it. Maybe it was just a mistake. He missed copying you on the mail, that's all.

Some of you will argue, 'You don't know him, he did it on purpose.' Perhaps. But that's a remote chance. A smaller possibility. Hanlon's razor helps you reset the default option in your head. It makes sure your starting premise is that people are good. People want to help you. Sure, they make mistakes; we all do. But the world is a good place. Try using Hanlon's razor, and you will discover that is indeed usually the case. And you will find the whole universe conspiring to make things happen the way you want them to.

Hanlon's razor will make you happier and make your world a better place too.

That banana seller is a good guy after all.

> Next time you fee hard done by, remember Hanlon's razor. Never attribute to malice that which can be explained by negligence. Or stupidity. Tell yourself it was an oversight, an unintended mistake. And it is not that the person—or the world—is conspiring against you. It will make you happier and your world a better place too.

For many years now, we've been told 'seeing is believing'. Maybe we were being told the wrong thing. Could it be that the reverse is in fact true? That ***believing is seeing****?*

Our mind plays these tricks on us. Once we believe something, everything we see seems to fit in with our beliefs. Our perception becomes our reality.

You could, of course, use this to your advantage. Change your thinking and your life will start to change. Change your mindset, change the way you look at your world and your world will begin to look different. Very different.

But watch out too. Other people could be leveraging this to change your thinking—so you start to see an altered reality. That happens too. More often than we imagine.

The Tenth Floor of the JW Marriott

The JW Marriott, near the airport in Mumbai, is a lovely hotel. Like you'd expect a JW Marriott to be.

Something interesting happened some time ago. I was there for a workshop I was conducting. The venue for our meeting was a lovely, well-lit room on the tenth floor. So every morning we'd troop up from the lobby to the tenth floor. Then head down to the café for lunch and head back up post a sumptuous meal.

After lunch on day two of the workshop, we headed back to our meeting room on the tenth floor. As we got out of the elevator, one of the participants remarked how marvellous the elevators were. They were so fast, it took no time to get from the lobby to floor number ten. And the elevators were so good that you didn't feel the sudden thrust of a jet taking off. It was a smooth, no-fuss ride that took us from the lobby to the tenth floor. And someone said you would expect nothing less from the fabulous folks at the Marriott. Indeed.

And then it hit us. Someone drew the curtain open in the room, to let some sunlight in. And as we looked out, we realized floor number ten wasn't actually the tenth floor. It was in fact the first floor of the hotel. The Marriott had just decided to refer to it as the tenth floor! Now many hotels take liberties with floor numbers. But I couldn't help thinking about how this simple renaming of floors impacted all of us. And our thinking.

We were quick to think how good the elevators were. And how magnificent the hotel was. All because we believed we were going from the lobby to the tenth floor. In a jiffy.

We see a variant of the tenth-floor phenomenon at work in our lives. Many organizations use a variant of the tenth-floor idea to keep employees happy. In the good old days, becoming the vice president of a company was a big deal. It usually took three decades of dedicated service to get to that exalted position. But those were the good old days. As times changed, people's expectations of growth and career velocity changed too. And many organizations responded by increasing the number of levels, to make sure employees got promoted faster and more often. So you could now become a VP before you turned thirty. Of course, post that, you would become executive VP. And then senior VP. And then . . . the list goes on. But truth be told, there was joy in being able to tell your mother-in-law that you'd become a VP at thirty.

Shopping on the Internet can give you a taste of this phenomenon too. You will find sellers offering you an online programme (or a book or a product) for a massive 90 per cent discount! So you pay only $9 for something that costs $99. Needless to say, chances are the seller woke up one morning and decided that the regular price would be $99. Ah, the joys of saving $90!

All of which goes to show that it's still true that our beliefs shape our reality. Thinking you are on the tenth floor can make you feel good about the view, the breeze and the elevator speeds too. Belief is big. We could all take a leaf out of the Marriott book and find ways of tweaking the world around us to help change beliefs. Other people's. And our own too.

Helping people see the world differently can be quite simple. As simple as renaming floor one as ten!

Beliefs shape our reality. Thinking you are on the tenth floor can make you feel good about the view, the breeze and the elevator speeds too. Belief is big. We could all take a leaf out of the Marriott book and find ways of tweaking the world around us to help change beliefs. Other people's. And our own too.

One of the bigger barriers clouding our judgement of people is the stereotypes in our heads. We all have these preconceived notions of people and things. And most times, we don't look at people with fresh eyes. We let the shorthand code of stereotypes influence our thinking. And mostly we are looking for cues that only reinforce the stereotype. Any evidence to the contrary is summarily dismissed.

It's a good idea to ***block the stereotypes in your head****. Everyone deserves a second chance. Start with a clean slate. And get ready to get surprised.*

They Are *All* Like That!

I am sure you will agree that all auto drivers are the same. All over the country. And here's what happened with us during a holiday in Kerala.

We had taken the train from Trivandrum to a town called Tripunithura, to visit a dear uncle and aunt. As we got off the train—around 8 p.m.—I pulled out my phone to book an Uber. Eleven minutes away, said the app. But after waiting—and waiting—I was told there were no cabs available. Same with Ola. And there were no autorickshaws around either. With a wife and three bags in tow, things were looking a bit grim.

And then an auto came by. 'Where to?' asked the driver. And when he learnt that my destination was only a kilometre away, he didn't seem too pleased. 'Hop in,' he said. He didn't start the meter. He didn't quote a fare. But I was glad to be on my way.

When we reached home, I got off and—in a display of gratitude and relief—gave the auto driver hundred bucks. The fare would have been Rs 25 or Rs 30, but I wanted to thank the guy for getting us home. And in any case, the cab fare would have been about the same! As he looked at the Rs 100 note in my hand, I was sure he would ask for more. Guess what the auto driver said?

He said, 'No, sir, that's a lot. Fifty rupees should be fine.' And I said, no, no, you were helpful, keep it. But he refused and insisted that I take the Rs 50 change. I had no choice.

As he drove away into the night, I couldn't help thinking what a good human being he was! I thought about how we have these stereotypes in our heads about people. We think of auto drivers as these wily chaps trying to cheat us off ten–twenty rupees. Maybe we all need to hit the reset button. And respect the fact that there is an honest, human being inside that auto driver's uniform.

As I thought about it later that night, I couldn't help thinking how we encounter the 'auto driver' ever so often. In our organizations, our communities, our lives. Someone we've built a false perception about. Someone we've wrongly condemned as untrustworthy. Someone we are convinced is out to get us. And we behave with these people in a manner that makes no secret of our distrust. Not only are we doing a disservice to those folks, we are also short-changing ourselves. We begin to be suspicious of innocent people. A train ride that could have meant new friends and fun conversations turns into a bore, because we don't want to strike up a conversation with a stranger. In dealing with a vendor, we treat him like a crook who is out to cheat us—and not a partner who could help us win. There are good people out there, waiting to help. But we are busy putting up a 'Do Not Disturb' sign.

A good idea, then, for each of us to demolish the demons of preconceived notions in our heads. Break the mould of that stereotype. Take fresh guard. There is goodness around us. People are generally trustworthy. You need to give humanity a chance. The world is indeed conspiring to help you succeed. Don't turn them away!

Change the way you think. And make your world a better place.

> We have these stereotypes in our heads about people. Maybe we all need to hit the reset button. We begin to be suspicious of innocent people. Not only are we doing a disservice to those folks, we are also short-changing ourselves. There are good people out there, waiting to help. But we are busy putting up a 'Do Not Disturb' sign.

Have you heard of confirmation bias? It's all around us and plagues our decision-making. Simply put, confirmation bias is our tendency to focus only on the evidence that fits our existing beliefs, and ignore the rest. Not because the evidence is weak, but because it doesn't match our thinking and our beliefs.

We see some evidence that supports our thinking and are quick to pronounce the verdict. Good idea to explore, seek more evidence, look for contra-indicators. And then decide. **Think again.** *That snap judgement you so proudly and quickly reached is often wrong. Good to realize that.*

The Day the Car Key Didn't Work

I knew it was a problem waiting to happen.

But let me start from the beginning. I had a car—an old Honda Accord—which only seemed to get better with age. It worked well, except for a minor problem. The door lock wouldn't open if you inserted the key. You had to use the remote. Not a big problem, because the remote-operated key worked well. The wife kept telling me to get it set right, but since I was not sure how much longer the car would remain with us, I kept putting it off. She'd warn me that one day the remote would stop working and I would get stuck. But I never thought that day would come.

It did.

I drove out one morning with my visiting five-year-old nephew to a neighbourhood toyshop. It was a treat the kid was looking forward to, and so was I. We parked the car and got off, and I pressed the remote to lock the car. But it wouldn't lock. I tried again. And again. Pressed harder. No luck. Damn, I said to myself. Did it have to happen now? Should have listened to the wife and got the lock and key set right. What now? I couldn't leave the car and go. The worried look on the kid's face suggested he knew the toy-buying expedition was in jeopardy. I banged the remote key on my palm, tried blowing at it to clean the dust, but nothing worked. I tried calling the service centre for help, but the calls went unanswered.

Then, as I walked to the other side of the car, I noticed that the rear window was open. And because the window glass was down, the car wasn't getting locked! That was all. I rolled up the window and bingo—the remote worked. With the car safely locked, we made our way to the toyshop. In the end, it was a fun, memorable day for the little fellow. And as I reflected on what had happened, it was a memorable day for me too.

Often, when things go wrong, we have an immediate hypothesis of what might have caused the problem. We are convinced that we know the problem. We don't look for fresh evidence or data points on what might have caused it. We get locked into the idea that's dominant in our heads. Our idea. We are quick to jump to conclusions.

Imagine your team is working on a new product launch. It's a fantastic product. Everyone's excited. You are concerned, though, that at this price there may not be enough takers. You push for a lower price. You get overruled. The launch happens with a lot of fanfare. Six months later, when results aren't quite what the business expected, you are sure you know why it's not working. And you are not surprised. It's the price, of course!

Truth is, the problem might lie elsewhere. Could it be that salespeople weren't able to explain the features? Or was service an issue? It's also a possibility that customers did not know about the product. But you have a solid, internal hypothesis about faulty pricing. And you don't give the real reason a chance to present itself.

Watch out. Next time you think you know what the problem is, pause. Keep an open mind as you look at what might have caused the problem.

Maybe someone's left the car window open.

> When things go wrong, we have an immediate hypothesis of what might have caused the problem. We don't look for fresh evidence or data points on what might have caused it. We get locked into the idea that's dominant in our heads. Truth is, the problem might lie elsewhere. Next time you think you know what the problem is, pause. Keep an open mind.

WHAT LEADERS DO

Winning in the game of life is a matter of give and take. Here's how. Learn to give credit to other people. And learn to take ownership.

Show gratitude. Never think it's only about you. Acknowledge the role other people play in your life's journey. And suddenly, you will find the whole world conspiring to help you succeed.

And take ownership. Don't look to blame other people. Take responsibility. When you do that, you remind yourself that the problem may appear big, but the solution is in your hands. That's hugely empowering.

Success is simple. Give and take.

Give credit, take ownership.

Give and Take: Lessons from the Miracle on the Hudson

It was a cold winter afternoon in January 2009. US Airways flight 1549 was all set for take-off from LaGuardia airport in New York to Charlotte. There were 155 people on board, including five members of the crew.

The co-pilot was in command as the plane took off. In less than two minutes, it had reached an altitude of about 2800 feet. And that was when passengers heard a sudden loud bang. They felt the plane shake. Some even saw flames coming from the engines. After that, a second bang. A thud. And an eerie silence.

What had happened was that birds—a flock of geese—had hit the engines of the plane, and both engines had packed up. Planes are designed in such a way that if one engine fails, no problem; but if both engines fail, big problem. Flight 1549 now had no power—it was a glider.

The captain immediately took control of the plane while the co-pilot tried to check the manuals to see what to do when both engines fail. The captain radioed air traffic control (ATC) at LaGuardia to tell them they have a problem. And the ATC at LaGuardia said, 'Come right back, we will clear the runway for you.' But the captain could sense there was not enough power left in the plane. He wasn't sure the plane would make it back to LaGuardia. He could see the traffic on the streets of Manhattan below him, and the boats on the Hudson River. He knew that if he did not make it back to the airport, the damage would be huge: 155 people in the plane, and several hundreds more on the streets below.

The captain was an experienced pilot, with over thirty years of flying under his belt. He considered landing at a lesser-used airstrip in New Jersey. But he gave that idea up, figuring he wouldn't make it. Time was running out. The plane was descending. That was when the captain—Captain Sullenberger—took a brave decision. He decided to land the plane in water, on the Hudson. In what has now come to be known as the 'miracle on the Hudson', Captain Sully landed the plane in water. And all 155 people came out alive.

Leadership pundits have often asked the question: What is it about leaders like Captain Sully that enables them to take such bold decisions? Several people cite Captain Sully's action as an example of a terrific leadership trait—a trait that is seen as a useful predictor of leadership success. And that trait is 'learning agility'. Put simply, learning agility is '*knowing what to do when you don't know what to do*'. It's the ability to synthesize past experiences and learnings. To solve new, never-before-seen problems. Learning agility is, in essence, what they don't teach you at B-school, or at flying school. But you learn by combining knowledge with experience from the school of hard knocks. Good idea, then, for all of us to hone our learning agility! Good to 'know what to do when you don't know what to do'.

There are two other lessons that we can all take away from Captain Sully's heroics on the Hudson. And both of these are exemplified by a couple of things he said during the episode.

Here's the first one. Remember who was in command when the plane took off? Yes, it was the co-pilot. But the minute the bird-hit happens, Captain Sully says, 'My aeroplane.' The co-pilot says, 'Your aeroplane,' and hands over the controls to his captain.

'My aeroplane.'

Two simple words but powerful from a leadership standpoint. Good leaders learn to take ownership in a crisis. They don't look for someone to blame. They don't panic. They don't complain about the birds or other external factors. They say, 'My aeroplane.' They take ownership. And that's something we all need to learn to do. Learn to say, 'My aeroplane.'

How do you respond when there's a crisis? When a problem occurs and the results aren't what you might expect? What do you do when you are in trouble? Do you look at your colleagues and try and find out who is to blame? Do you distance yourself from the problem? And leave your struggling team-mates to resolve the crisis all by themselves? Do you blame it on the environment, on the birds?

Or do you, like captain Sully, take ownership? As a leader, you owe it to your team—and to yourself—to take charge, and to be seen to be in charge, when a crisis hits. Good leaders are quick to take control. They almost seem to relish the challenge. The prospect of failure does not cross their minds. The 'My aeroplane' attitude in problem situations is something all of us would do well to adopt. Get that mindset of taking ownership. Say, 'My aeroplane.'

Then there's the second lesson. And that's after Captain Sully has landed the plane on the Hudson. And all the passengers have been evacuated. As you would expect, Captain Sully is the last man to emerge. The waiting media folks and the TV crews hail the captain as a hero and give him credit for saving so many lives. 'You are a hero, captain,' is what they all seem to be saying. But Captain Sully is quick to point out that he isn't a hero. He turns to his crew and says, 'They did it!'

He gives credit to his co-pilot, Jeff Skiles, and to the three women who formed the cabin crew, Donna, Sheena and Doreen, superwomen who held their nerve and did a fantastic job under pressure. Captain Sully even thanks the ferry operators and the chopper crews for their help.

'They did it!'

Good idea for us, too, to be the kind of leaders who give credit. Sometimes, we worry that if we give others credit, people wouldn't even know that we were responsible. Don't worry. Give credit. That old rule still holds. The more you give, the more you get.

We all need to learn to say these words more often: 'My aeroplane' and 'They did it'. Two simple statements that encapsulate two stellar traits of good leaders: They take ownership in a crisis, and they give credit.

Now here's the interesting bit. It is not as if we haven't learnt to say 'My aeroplane' and 'They did it'. We make both these statements. Often. It's just that we get the timing mixed up. So, when things go wrong, we say, 'They did it!' And after the problem is solved and all is well, we say, 'My aeroplane!'

Good idea, then, to get Captain Sully's learning agility. And good idea, too, to be the kind of leader who says 'My aeroplane' and 'They did it'.

And yes, don't get the timing mixed up.

> We all need to learn to say these words more often: 'My aeroplane' and 'They did it'. Two simple statements that encapsulate two stellar traits of good leaders: They take ownership in a crisis, and they give credit. And yes, remember not to get the timing mixed up.

If you are a team leader, there are two ways you could look at your role.

One is by focusing on how many people report to you. That seems to immediately convey a position of power and authority. The image of a ruler—or a leader—with several people waiting to obey your command. Many of us see our roles like that. And we love that feeling of authority and power that comes with it.

There's another way you could look at that role. How many people are you responsible for? How many people do you need to help achieve their goals?

People reporting to you versus people you are responsible for.

Think about it.

Servant leadership is a powerful idea. Remember, you are ***servant, not master****.*

The Upside-Down Organization Chart

You've seen it before. That standard slide in a corporate presentation that shows the organization structure.

A familiar pyramid it is. The boss at the top, the vice presidents below him, followed by the general managers and so on. At the bottom of that organization chart is the army of foot soldiers who stand and deliver—the company's salesmen.

But that was not quite what I saw when my mentor and former boss Suman Sinha—then the CEO of PepsiCo India—presented the org chart. It looked upside-down. You must remember those were pre-PowerPoint days, with 35 mm slides and carousel projectors. And I thought some rookie trainee would lose his job for inserting the slide upside-down.

Suman was quick to explain that the upside-down org chart wasn't a mistake. It was deliberate. He was building an upside-down organization.

'At the top of this organization are our salespeople,' he said. 'They are closest to our customers. And they know best what this organization needs to do to delight our customers. They decide what we do. Below the sales guys are a bunch of managers whose job it is to ensure that the salesmen get all the support they need. Below those managers are a set of general managers. Their job is to mobilize resources to make sure the sales teams get what they need. Below them are the VPs, whose job it is to make sure their functional teams are supporting the sales effort. And do you see that guy at the bottom of the pyramid? That's me. The CEO. My job is simple. I need to ensure that the organization is geared to support the salespeople.'

Wow! On that single slide, you could see a leader striving to build an organization with a difference. A frontline-focused organization that was determined to win with customers. Not a company where everyone was looking 'upwards' to see what the boss wanted done, but an organization where everyone was looking outwards, to understand what the customer wanted done.

And that made a difference. A small change in the org chart made a big difference to the company's culture.

Are you looking to create a customer-focused organization? You may want to invert your organization too. Make your salesperson the hero. Make the customer your God. And make sure everyone's looking outwards, not inwards. Traditional organization structures are designed for control, ensuring that we create hurdles. We make it difficult for salespeople to serve their customers. The typical pyramid-structured organizations are engineered to do what the boss wants, not what the customer wants.

In one stroke, Suman created an empowered frontline. There was respect for the salesman. The sales folks all began to walk a wee bit taller. They loved the attention, trust and responsibility that seemed to come with it. Soon, commercial teams were getting quicker at processing the sales team's proposals. And their expense statements too. Factory teams began to listen a little more intently to what the sales teams were saying. Customer complaints and feedback moved up to the top of the agenda. The magic had begun.

This change in the org structure—nay, the change in the culture itself—wasn't only about having a fancy slide in a presentation. It was a message that Suman ensured was driven home. Take, for instance, what happened at a launch conference for the sales team in Lucknow. As Suman got on to the stage to address the team, guess who was seated in the front rows? You are right: All the senior leaders who had flown in from the corporate headquarters. They were in the VIP seats! Isn't that always the case, in every company, every conference, every city? The salesmen—the real folks for whom the launch conference was intended—were all at the back. Suman got them to swap places. The senior folks went to the back of the room. The salesmen, the folks who drove those Pepsi trucks, took their seats in the front rows. When a sales army is made to feel as special as this one did, magic happens. You can bet they will do everything they can—and a little bit more—to make sure they come out winning. And they did.

So if you are looking to create an empowered, frontline-focused, passionate organization, look no further.

Take the first step. Turn your organization upside-down.

> Looking to create a customer-focused business? Build an upside-down organization. Make your salesperson the hero. Make sure it is not a company where everyone is looking 'upwards' to see what the boss wants done, but an organization where everyone is looking outwards, to understand what the customer wants done.

Good leaders make sure they know their business. Cold. They know what's happening, they know what works. And they know why.

Better leaders go one step further. They know their people too. Their strengths and weaknesses, their aspirations and fears.

How do they do that?

Not by reading a set of annual appraisals, nor by asking HR for an assessment report. They do that by spending time getting to know the talent in the team. By watching them in action. Speaking with them. Hearing them out.

To be a better leader, make it your priority: ***Know your people****. Firsthand.*

How Well Do You Know Your People?

A Century Is Not Enough. That's the title of Sourav Ganguly's autobiography. It's the story of a cricketer who was arguably India's finest Test captain and, without a doubt, the man who instilled the belief in the Indian team that they could win—anywhere in the world.

When Sourav was going around the country launching his book, I got lucky. Symbiosis Institute of Business Management (SIBM) were hosting the Pune book launch. They invited me to host a conversation with Sourav, to talk to him about the book and about the lessons it might have for the budding leaders at the business school.

We spoke about leadership. About his problems with coach Greg Chapell. About mind games. And about team spirit and 'Dadagiri'. My favourite segment from that conversation? The bit where we spoke about leaders backing young talent. Several cricketers from that era have spoken glowingly about the role their captain played in their success. Zaheer Khan and Virender Sehwag.

Yuvraj Singh and Harbhajan Singh. They have all talked about how they owe their success to Sourav—a captain who backed them, believed in them and gave them the opportunities to succeed.

As any leader will tell you, backing young talent can be a risky proposition. What if it doesn't make good? If the person fails to deliver, the leader could be accused of bias, even favouritism. So my question to Sourav was straight: How did he stick his neck out and back those guys? Wasn't he scared of what might happen if they didn't click?

Sourav's answer was simple. 'You need to know your players,' he said. 'You've got to get close and see the talent firsthand. If you don't do that, and you only go by what others say—or worse, by what the scoreboard says—you are always unsure. If you don't know them, you can't back them. Knowing the talent is a captain's responsibility—not the selectors' job. And when you back those young guns, they will do everything they can—and more—to repay that confidence.'

That, I thought, was great advice for all leaders. Know your talent. Knowing your people is your job—not HR's job. The quality of your decisions as a leader depends on how well you know your people. Indeed, your success as a leader depends on that.

So when Sourav saw Harbhajan Singh bowling in the nets, he didn't see his first-class record. He did not see how many wickets he had taken in domestic cricket. He saw a talented off-spinner. Sourav saw a spark in Harbhajan's eyes that showed him how much he wanted to succeed. And he saw a mind that was plotting the next dismissal. He saw a potential match-winner and backed him, knowing Harbhajan would make good. And he did.

Listening to Sourav, I was reminded of something my former boss Suman Sinha did as the CEO at PepsiCo. The annual performance appraisal process was taken very seriously at PepsiCo, far more than in most other organizations. And guess what the highlight of the performance appraisal season was? Suman Sinha's insistence on discussing the performance of even the junior managers in the company. Suman wanted to know how all the assistant managers were doing. He wanted to hear about the future leaders, and he wanted to get to know them better.

He would have his leadership team, too, sit in on the appraisal discussions. Along with the HR folks, of course. Appraisal meetings would often spill into the wee hours of the morning. But Suman was happy doing that. You might think a CEO has more important things to do. That he should not be spending time discussing a junior manager in some corner of the country. But that was not how Suman looked at it. For him, it was important to get to know his people. He would ask questions, push and probe and try and understand the person. In many cases, he would try and connect the discussion to his memories of a visit to a factory, or to a market visit, or to a time when he would have interacted with that person. The message was clear. For this leader, the person was not about targets and achievements and ratings alone. He was interested in getting to know the person behind those numbers. Result? He would make bold bets on young talent, because over the years he got to know his people well. Really well.

People often talk about the paucity of talent in organizations these days. And about how good young leaders are hard to come by. Maybe we are getting it wrong. The problem is not that there is a scarcity of talent. It's just that leaders aren't investing time in getting to know their people.

Be a Sourav. Or a Suman. Make that extra effort to know your people. Watch them play. Sit in on appraisal discussions. Do field visits. And skip-level meetings. Remember, good leaders make an effort to know their people.

You should too.

> Know your talent. Knowing your people is your job—not HR's job. The quality of your decisions as a leader depends on how well you know your people. Indeed, your success as a leader depends on that.

Remember the terror attack at the Taj some years ago? It was a long night, hard to forget.

The senior leadership team of a large successful company was meeting there that night. And they spent several hours holed up in their meeting room while the mayhem continued in the corridors and other parts of the hotel. In the wee hours of the next morning, help arrived, and they were all able to climb down through a window to safety. Every single one of them: the leaders and their spouses too.

And guess who was the last man to leave the room? Yes, you are right. It was indeed the CEO.

Captains of ships—and good leaders—know this. ***It is not about me. It is about them.*** *Always.*

People first.

The Unlucky Guy in the Queue

Long queues at the airport security check can be frustrating. But as I discovered at Bengaluru airport some years ago, the queue can throw up interesting lessons too.

I remember it was early morning, and the airport was crowded. All the baggage-screening machines were operational, and there were multiple queues out there. I picked the line that seemed the shortest. And as it invariably happens, from that moment on, it seemed to be the one moving slowest. As we neared the baggage scanner, I noticed there were very few laptop trays left at the front of our queue. But the adjacent machine had a huge pile of trays.

I did a quick count of the trays lying in front: there were seven. Then, instinctively, I counted the number of people ahead of me and was delighted to discover that there were exactly six people in front. Seven trays. And I was the seventh guy. Lucky me, I said to myself even as a smile escaped my lips. I knew it was no big deal. But who wants to get to the front and then have to wait, shout out to the security guy and request him for trays, and wait till someone comes along and piles up the trays again?

I couldn't help but look at the man behind me in the queue. The unlucky guy, the man who would have to wait for a tray.

Each of the folks in front picked up a tray, and I watched intently as they put their laptops and their phones and wallets away. When my turn came, there it was. The last tray. I picked it up with a sense of triumph. I put my laptop on it and pushed it on to the conveyor belt. Then I turned for one last look at what the man behind me might be feeling.

Guess what he did?

The man behind me, that unlucky guy, walked across to pick up a tray from the large pile of trays at the adjacent machine. With both hands, he picked up not one but about a dozen trays and brought them to where our queue was. He was sorted. As were several people behind him.

What a guy, I thought to myself. I knew I had just seen a demonstration of true leadership in action. In that instant, I got a masterclass in what great leaders are all about. And what good human beings do. Their instinct is to focus not on themselves and their own needs, but on other people and what they might need. They have a desire to care for—and help—the people around them.

As I cleared security, I couldn't help thinking how we tend to get caught up with ourselves. We want to get ahead in the queue. We want that last tray. We don't want to be left behind. Maybe we should all pause and take a leaf out of that young man's book. Focus on others. Help other people. Care.

Long queues at airports can be boring. But as I discovered, sometimes they can teach us powerful lessons that stay with us forever.

And yes, if you were the man behind me in the queue that day, thank you, stranger, for that lesson in what leadership is all about. And for showing me what good people do.

Leadership is not about me. It's about them. Always was. Always will be.

> Good leaders focus not on themselves and their own needs, but on other people and what they might need. They have a desire to care for—and help—the people around them. Leadership is not about me. It's about them.

A colleague calls you and asks you for directions to your favourite restaurant. 'From the main road, do I take the left turn, or do I turn right?' Since you go there often and know the place well, you tell her to take the right.

But you forget something important. Which way you should be going depends on where you are coming from.

And this happens often in our lives.

What should you do? How do you do it? What's the right thing to do? Important questions. We are all looking for answers.

And we all have our views. Views that are based on what has worked for us, or on what we believe is right. Because we take the right turn every time, we are convinced it is the thing to do.

Pause. And consider this. ***Which way you should be going depends on where you are.***

What's the Starting Point?

Imagine you are the head of a country's treasury, and you are tasked with increasing the government's tax revenues. You have a simple decision to make. Would you increase taxes to increase revenue? Or would you lower the tax rate to increase revenues? What would you do?

To answer the question, you might want to turn to the Laffer curve, named after the American economist Arthur Laffer. But first, an interesting story of how Laffer's curve was born.

The year was 1974. Dick Cheney and Donald Rumsfeld—both senior officials in President Gerald Ford's staff—were at a restaurant with Laffer, who was then a professor of economics at the University of Chicago. They were discussing President Ford's tax policy. The linear relationship between revenue and tax was easy for all to see (more tax, more revenue). But Prof. Laffer had a different point to make.

He pulled out a napkin and drew two axes: the X-axis was the tax rate and on the Y-axis was total revenue. He then showed that when the tax rate is 0 per cent, tax revenue is zero. And if the tax rate was to be 100 per cent, the revenue would again be zero. Because no one would have any incentive to work and earn money if all of it, in any case, was to go to the government. The professor then drew a parabola, which started at zero and ended at zero, and that came to be known as Laffer's curve.

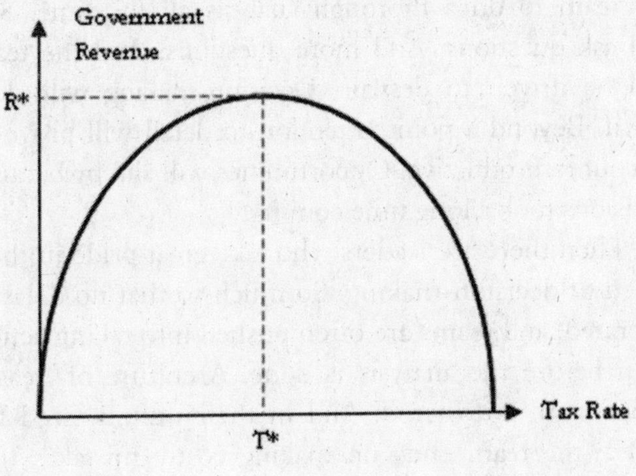

Laffer showed that the relationship between tax rate and revenue is non-linear. And that for every tax rate, there is another tax rate on that curve that will get you the same revenue. As you increase the tax rate, the revenue increases—up to a point. And then, after the point where revenue is maximized, it begins to decline. A further increase in the tax rate results in a lowering of the revenue. So to increase revenue, whether you should increase tax or lower it depends on where you are on the curve! And that's at the heart of the idea of non-linear thinking. Which way you should go depends on where you are to start with. That's something leaders would do well to remember.

Often, leaders make the mistake of falling in love with their ideas and philosophies. They push those ideas to an extreme—to their own detriment. So a leader who is enamoured of, say, her attention to detail will push her team to do a thorough analysis all the time. She will ask questions. And more questions. And the team will be driven to despair. Decision-making will slow down. Beyond a point, attention to detail will prove to be counterproductive. Opportunities will slip by because decisions took a long time coming.

Then there are leaders who take great pride in their speed of decision-making. So much so that no delay is tolerated, and teams are often pushed into taking action even before the analysis is done. A culture of 'ready, shoot, aim' is fostered. And in their unholy need for speed, the team ends up making costly mistakes that often spell their ruin.

The point is simple. Attention to detail is good, but up to a point. And the speed of decision-making is good too, up to a point. Too much of either can be a bad thing. That's true for most leadership challenges as well. Profit maximization or sales growth? Hard taskmaster or chilled-out, easy-going boss? As a leader, it's a good idea to remember the Laffer curve. Remember, at both ends of the Laffer curve, the revenue is zero. And there are always two ways of getting the same results.

Think non-linear. In life and in business, which way you need to go depends on where you are to start with.

Think about it.

Which way you should go depends on where you are to start with. That's something leaders would do well to remember. And there are always two ways of getting the same results.

'Our biggest assets walk out of the office every day.' You've probably heard that line before. Leaders often talk about people as their biggest assets. But do they also walk the talk?

If you believe people are your biggest assets, take care of them. ***Invest in your people.*** *Show your commitment.*

People. The best investment you can make. In good times and bad.

Coffee Breaks Are Good

Something interesting happened on 26 February 2008. All Starbucks cafes across the United States were closed that evening.

It was termed the most expensive coffee break in corporate history. And yet, several people cite it as one of the finest examples of a business leader making a statement and walking the talk on people development. Whichever way you look at it, the events of that day in February 2008 hold a valuable lesson for leaders.

As the clock struck five that evening, all 7100 Starbucks stores in the United States began to down their shutters. A little note posted on the doors of each of those outlets politely informed customers: 'We're taking time to perfect our espresso. Great espresso requires practice. That's why we're dedicating ourselves to honing our craft.'

In the hours that followed, all 135,000 Starbucks baristas got trained on how to prepare the perfect espresso. That's not all. They also got a powerful reminder of the reason why they existed and what made Starbucks special. They learnt to make the perfect brew. And they all heard their CEO talking to them—straight from the heart. Not just about making great coffee but also about making Starbucks great again.

The move cost Starbucks $6 million in lost sales and labour costs. Imagine shutting down the business and turning away customers—all for a training programme! If you were the CEO, would you have done that?

Critics and competitors had a field day. Some experts said that by shutting the stores for training, Starbucks was admitting to their customers that there was a problem. Newspaper pundits and TV show hosts went to town, 'roasting' Starbucks for the store closure. Everyone seemed to be saying it was a 'Grande' mistake.

Everyone? Well, not quite. Howard Schultz, the charismatic CEO of Starbucks, was convinced that they had done the right thing. 'How could it be wrong to invest in your people?' he reasoned. Schultz knew that for Starbucks to rediscover its mojo, they needed to train their baristas—in the shortest possible time. When someone suggested that they shut all stores to train the entire team, all at once, it sounded crazy. Risky. Preposterous even. What would people say? What would be the cost? How would Wall Street react? For Schultz, none of that mattered. What mattered was the desperate need to get the magic back, and to make sure the team got the training, and the self-belief, they needed. Schultz followed his heart and shut all stores.

Events over the subsequent months confirmed that the move worked well for Starbucks. Quality scores for their coffee went up. Customer satisfaction scores climbed. And best of all, the morale in the organization skyrocketed. Employees were thrilled to be part of a team where the leader was willing to take such bold, decisive action.

Ten years later, Starbucks had a problem of a different kind. It wasn't about the coffee. It was about ensuring that their staff made all customers feel welcome, without any bias. The need for sensitivity training was sparked off by an unfortunate incident at a Starbucks in Philadelphia. And what did Starbucks do? You guessed right: they shut all 8000 stores in the US for a few hours on 29 May 2018, to train their staff. All 175,000 people.

'People are our biggest strength' is an oft-repeated cliché. It is quite fashionable for leaders to say that. But when it comes to investing in training and developing that resource, how do leaders fare? Not too well. Haven't you heard of a training programme being rescheduled because it was a month-end or a quarter-close? 'We have targets to deliver' is the excuse. How often has a senior leader skipped the scheduled session in a training programme because 'something more important' cropped up? Does all this sound uncomfortably familiar?

Maybe we should all take a leaf out of Howard Schultz's book. In our frenzy to grow, and our desire to demonstrate that we mean business, we often sacrifice people development at the altar of urgency and short-term gains. Don't do that. Don't pay lip service to people development. Abraham Lincoln had sensible advice for business leaders—many, many years ago—when he said, 'If I had six weeks to chop down a tree, I would spend the first four weeks sharpening the saw.' As a leader in a hurry, make sure you aren't forgetting to sharpen the saw. It's also hugely energizing for an organization when a leader does dramatic stuff to make a point. Schultz did that with the store closure. When was the last time you did a Howard Schultz?

Invest in your people. Make a bold statement. Time, then, for leaders to wake up and smell the coffee.

> We often sacrifice people development at the altar of urgency and short-term gains. Don't do that. Don't pay lip service to people development. Abraham Lincoln had sensible advice for business leaders—many, many years ago—when he said, 'If I had six weeks to chop down a tree, I would spend the first four weeks sharpening the saw.'

Checklists are fabulous. And as Dr Atul Gawande showed in his book on the subject, they can be used across various fields to improve outcomes. The challenge, though, is that checklists can take time. And that's something we may not always have.

Which is why leaders develop an intuitive sense-check—a lead indicator of sorts—that helps them feel the pulse and know what's happening.

You don't always have the liberty of running through an entire checklist to know what's happening. A sense-check can do the trick. ***Build your own sense-check.***

The Curious Case of the Brown M&M's

Have you heard of a rock band called Van Halen? They were quite popular in the '80s. Even if you haven't heard of them, there's an interesting little story about the band that you must know—a story that offers a useful tip for leaders.

Like most big performers, Van Halen too had elaborate contracts with the event management companies they worked with. The contract would have all the details of their requirements—types of lighting, sound, the flooring, the microphones, even the length of the wiring required. And tucked away somewhere in their fifty-three-page contract was a rather strange clause: Van Halen required the organizers to place a large bowl of M&M's (those colourful button-like chocolate candies) backstage—but with all the brown M&M's removed. Imagine. A bowl full of M&M's. But no brown M&M's!

Stars and celebrities are known to make outlandish demands, and you would be excused for thinking that this 'no brown M&M's' request is one more example of starry behaviour. Not quite. As David Lee Roth, the band's lead singer and guitarist, explained, there was good reason why their contracts included this rather ludicrous request.

Van Halen wanted to make sure the organizers had taken care of all the details to make sure the audience enjoyed the performance. They would want the sound and lighting to be right. The stage had to be strong enough to take the weight of the heavy equipment that would be placed there. But how would Van Halen know that it had all been taken care of?

Simple. All they had to do was check the bowl of M&M's backstage. If there were no brown M&M's, they knew the event managers had read every clause in the contract and taken care of every detail. If there were brown M&M's—that spelt trouble. They would need to go over every detail once more to make sure all the requirements for the audience's enjoyment and safety had been taken care of. One quick look at the bowl of M&M's was all it took for them to know if the event manager had done all those little things essential for a great stage performance!

Great leaders have their own versions of the 'no brown M&M's' rule. They have a quick sense-check, a lead indicator, that tells them how things are.

Remember Ray Kroc? He was the man credited with building the global McDonald's franchise. The story goes that every time Ray visited a McDonald's, the first thing he would do was go into the washroom at the restaurant. Looking at the cleanliness of the loo, he could tell how well the franchisee was running the business! He didn't have to look at food audit reports and customer feedback scores and fancy PowerPoint presentations to know how business was. The washroom test was a good indicator of the overall health of the business.

As a young sales manager in the FMCG business, I had a boss who would take one look at the 'Route Book' in a distributor's godown—and he would know all about how the distributor was doing in the marketplace. You probably know of a leader who would visit a factory and check the workmen's canteen, or the scrapyard, or the cobwebs in the fans—to know how well the plant was being run.

Time then to find your own little sense-check. Your own lead indicator. So, what's your 'no brown M&M's' rule?

In life as in business, it's a good idea to have a quick sense-check, a lead indicator, that tells you how things are. So, what's your version of the 'no brown M&M's' rule? If you don't have one, develop it. And make it your own.

There are several stories about the greatness of Abraham Lincoln. And my favourite one is this.

The story goes that President Lincoln was polishing his shoes one morning, getting ready to go to work. A member of his senate walked into his chamber and was surprised to see the president polishing his own shoes. 'Mr President,' he exclaimed, 'you polish your own shoes?'

The President smiled and calmly said, 'Yes. But tell me whose shoes do you polish?'

Good leaders are like that. They are perfectly comfortable rolling up their sleeves and doing the dirty work. And more importantly, they will never ask a colleague to do something they wouldn't do themselves.

When they see a small problem that they can set right, they do it. No task is too small for a leader. ***No fuss, no ego.*** *Be that kind of leader.*

The Chairman's White Handkerchief

It happened over three decades ago, at a *kirana* shop in a corner of the country. It's a story that's been retold to successive generations of young managers at Hindustan Unilever. It's a story that bears repetition.

The chairman of the company was on a market visit in a small town in Kerala. At one store, he noticed a tin of Dalda (a popular brand of vanaspati at that time) on a corner shelf. As he reached out to take a closer look at the tin, he was horrified to see a thick layer of dust on the lid. There were sheepish looks on the faces of the folks accompanying the chairman. It wasn't something they wanted the chairman to see. The sales team's routine included cleaning stocks on the shelf—with particular attention to food products. This was a bad miss.

And what did the chairman do? Scream and shout? Threaten to sack someone? Talk about the need for better execution? Nope.

He put his hand into his trouser pocket, pulled out a clean, white handkerchief and proceeded to wipe the Dalda tin clean. That was it. He did what any foot soldier of the company might have done. It was about getting a job done, rather than worrying about whose job it was.

The sales team got the message, of course. Far better than they might have had the chairman shown anger and disappointment. The retailer's respect for the company went up a few notches in that instant too. All those present that day got a masterclass in leadership. And as the story got retold over the years, young managers began to understand what a leader's work ethic ought to be. And what great leadership looks like.

I was reminded of the Dalda and the handkerchief story once again several decades later. I was in a meeting with the managing director of a large auto ancillary company. With him was his head of Learning and Development. We sat around a little roundtable at their guesthouse. As the L&D head began the discussion, I saw the managing director get up and go into the kitchen. And he was back in a jiffy, with a cleaning cloth in his hand. He then went on to wipe the table clean. And as he saw the look of surprise on our faces, he said that when he put his diary on the table, he figured the table was dusty, and so he decided to clean it.

Now this is such a rare sight, I thought to myself. When was the last time you saw the managing director of a company actually take a mop out and clean a table—in front of a group of other people?

Think about it. He could have so easily done something else. He could have called out to the attendant, who at that stage was busy making some tea and coffee for us, and said, 'Come, I want you to clean the table right now!' Or he could have shouted at him for not having maintained a clean table. Or he could have complained about the world we live in and said, 'Look, there's so much dust around us!' He didn't do any of those. He was a man who had seen a problem (which none of us had actually noticed) and then decided, 'Hey, let me do something about it!' He went out, got a cloth and cleaned the table.

Great leaders are like that.

It is the kind of leadership that's becoming so rare to find in our world today. And it's also the kind of leadership that we all need to see more of. And *show* more of.

The chairman did it. The managing director did it. What's stopping you? What's your excuse? The next time you see a problem—when you see dust on the table or on your company's products—which nobody else has noticed, don't leave it there. Don't shout. Don't ask someone to set it right. Take a cloth and clean it!

Not only will you have a clean table—and clean products—but you'll also become a role model for others, exemplifying what great leadership looks like.

And, many years later, they will still be telling your story.

> When you see a problem that you can fix, fix it. Get the job done. Don't worry about whose job it is. Roll up your sleeves. Dirty your hands. You will earn the respect of your team. And you will set an example for them.

Everyone has a goal. Most businesses have goals too. But have you considered what you would do once you get there? What should we do after we have reached the peak and found the success we had set out to achieve?

Not everyone has a plan for that. Maybe we should.

Make sure you have an answer to the question, ***'After success, what?'***

Failing to Conquer Mount Everest

'29,000 feet!'

I still recall that moment several years ago when I shouted out that answer. At an interschool quiz contest. The question, as you might have guessed, was, 'What is the height of Mount Everest?'

I am not sure if it was the memory of that joyous moment that started off my fascination with Mount Everest. While I haven't come close to ever climbing to the top of the world's highest mountain, I have often written about it. And I have been fascinated by the lessons it might hold for all of us.

Mount Everest has often been used as a metaphor for getting to the top. For winning. And for becoming the best in class. John Buchanan, former coach of the Australian cricket team, used it too. Climbing Everest was the framework for his masterplan to take Australia to the top. He didn't do too badly, did he? Australia won the World Cup three times and became the No. 1 team under his watch.

Stories of Tenzing and Hillary have inspired generations of mountain-climbers to push themselves to take on the challenge, brave adversity and get to the top. Not everybody who starts the climb makes it back alive, though, and that only adds to the lure of the challenge. In recent years, there has often been a traffic jam on the road to Everest. And maybe that says something about the world we live in. Climbing Everest is still a tough challenge. But a mix of greed, willing agents and eager-beaver climbers have made it even riskier. Result? Several people attempt the expedition every year without the requisite training and preparation.

A recent study of failed missions to Mount Everest came up with an interesting finding. Eighty-five per cent of the deaths at Everest expeditions took place when the climbers were on their way down. Think about it. We all know climbing Mount Everest is tough, very tough. But no one told us that climbing down could be even more dangerous!

And that set me thinking. What explains this strange statistic? Why do more people die on the way down than on the climb up? Why do people falter after accomplishing the most difficult challenge? Everyone talks about climbing Mount Everest. Nobody talks about climbing down from there. But they should.

There's a lesson here. Organizations and individuals, all make plans on how to win, how to be successful and how to be the best in the world. But we also need to plan for what we will do *after* we get there. We need to have a plan for climbing down Mount Everest.

We all think of Everest as this hard-to-reach goal. We build strategies to overcome the terrain and the obstacles. We build perseverance, tell ourselves that we mustn't give up, even if the goal seems far. But we don't think too much about what we will do after we get there, do we? Is it this lack of planning that spells doom? Or is it that the euphoria of success makes us drop our guard and become careless, causing us to fail? You've reached the summit, hoisted the flag, the dream has come true. And then, the slip.

Some experts have pointed out that the way down from the peak of Mount Everest is in fact a treacherous path. In some ways, that's true of our lives too. Except no one has told us that. Business strategy documents and vision statements, they all talk about the goal. About where we want to go, how we will get there, and the metrics and milestones we will use to monitor progress. But they don't talk about what we will do once we get there. We are all missing an important piece.

Consider, for instance, the food service business. Everyone dreams of opening a restaurant! But it is a well-known fact that the restaurant business is a tough, tricky one. Mortality rates are high. It's like climbing Mount Everest. And I am sure you know of a restaurant in your neighbourhood that nailed it. They did the hard yards, got it right and became a hit. People queued up to get a table. And then suddenly, things started to go south. Maybe the service standards fell as the crowds swelled. Or maybe it was the rapid price increase, led by arrogance and greed. Or the decline in food quality after the chef left to start his own place. Whatever. The shutters came down, and the restaurant vanished.

In the razzmatazz of Bollywood, a million hopefuls come in hoping to get it right. Everyone wants to be a star, a superstar even. Rajesh Khanna, for instance, was the first real superstar, a phenomenon. But what happened after he reached the top makes for a sad story. Poor choices. Bad decisions. A group of yes-men who wouldn't tell the emperor he had no clothes on. And the refusal to face the reality meant a sharp fall from superstardom. How his fans wished his life's script were a bit different.

And this happens in business too. Think Kodak and Blockbuster. Or even Jet Airways. Their tales would have been different if their plans had included a section on getting down safe!

Good to remember what John F. Kennedy said way back in 1961 to inspire a nation. He talked of his dream 'of landing a man on the moon and returning him safely to the earth'. Notice, not just landing a man on the moon, but returning him safe to the earth too. It was a dream that came true when Neil Armstrong set foot on the moon eight years later. Everyone knew that 'landing a man on the moon' was a tough challenge. But success, as Kennedy was quick to point out, was not about landing a man on the moon. It was also about bringing him back alive.

It's time to add one more chapter to your strategic plans. And your goal-setting exercises too. We need to answer the question, 'What will we do after we get there?' What do we need to do to ensure that we get to the top of Mount Everest, and come back alive? That can be the secret to ensuring business longevity and success.

It is not surprising that Mount Everest continues to inspire the world. It is the ultimate symbol of peak achievement. But as you craft your own Everest vision statement, make sure there's a 'down to earth' element to it.

Climb up. And climb down safe too.

Everyone talks about climbing Mount Everest. Nobody talks about climbing down from there. But we should. We all have a lesson to learn.

We make plans on how to win, how to be successful and how to be the best in the world. But we also need to plan for what we will do *after* we get there. We need to have a plan for climbing down Mount Everest.

When we look at someone successful, it's easy to admire the talent and skill that got them there. We rave about their unique abilities.

But we don't always talk about the opportunities they got to show their talent. Performers need a stage. ***Talent needs opportunity.***

Good leaders recognize that. As they look at their success, they retain the humility to acknowledge the role that opportunity played in their success. They know there may have been smarter folks who missed out on the same opportunities.

And that's not all. As leaders, they recognize that they have a responsibility—to provide opportunities to raw talent.

Be that kind of leader.

Talent Needs Opportunity

Few people have captured the public imagination quite like A.B. de Villiers. He is a cricketer who is loved not only in his home country, South Africa, but also around the world.

There's an interesting little story that AB loves to share, about his early days as a schoolboy cricketer. It is a story that holds a valuable lesson for leaders. For parents too. Even if you are not a cricket fan, it's a story you must hear. A story of two men: A.B. de Villiers. And a man they called 'French'.

AB says there were several people who had a hand in his development as a cricketer. His parents, his coaches. Senior cricketers like Graeme Smith, Jacques Kallis and Mark Boucher. All of whom had a strong influence on AB. There was one other name in that list, not quite as well known: Francois Geldenhuys. The man they called 'French'. AB says that French was the man who backed him when he was most in need. He was the man who had a pivotal influence on AB's life and career. So what exactly did French do?

Flashback, then, to the year 2000. French was captain of the North Transvaal Schools team in a local interschool tournament. AB was in that team, and the coach had put him down to bat at No. 7—not a position where you can do much as a batsman. French spoke to the coach and said AB should be given a chance to open the innings. The coach agreed, even if somewhat reluctantly. AB grabbed the opportunity with both hands and scored a century. That hundred resulted in AB getting picked for the South Africa Colts team. He then got picked for the South Africa schools team a year later, and so on. And on.

Which raises the question: Would AB have made that kind of progress had French not spoken up at that time? What might have happened had AB been left to languish down the order at No. 7? We'll never know.

But as AB himself says, what we do know is this: There are several talented sportsmen out there who don't get to realize their full potential. They languish in obscurity. Simply because they don't get a chance to show their skills and capabilities. AB got his chance because someone spoke up. And that made all the difference.

That's true for sport, as well as for business and life. For every rising star in the world, there are several others who unfortunately never get a chance to prove their worth. Equally talented, as capable but deprived of the opportunity. Success is about talent. *And* about opportunity. When talent meets opportunity, history gets made.

If you think about it, you would see that this applies to your own life too. Your success, your achievements in life, are thanks to a mentor or a boss who took a chance on you and gave you a break. A break that allowed you to show what you were all about. Maybe they made you area sales manager, even though there were other more experienced candidates. And people were saying you weren't ready for it. Or someone promoted you out of turn to vice president, to head a business which you then rapidly grew. So even as you take pride in your talents and your achievements, take a moment to thank the men and women who gave you that opportunity.

More importantly, remember that now it's your turn to return the favour. Take a bet on raw talent. Bet on unripe fruit.

If you are a team leader, wishing you had an A.B. de Villiers in your team, you need to pause and think. Maybe there is already an AB in the team—but he hasn't got an opportunity to show what he is capable of. Give him a chance, please. Don't focus only on your established stars. Give young talent an opportunity.

As a leader—and star performer—you might wish you were an A.B. de Villiers, scoring runs, dazzling fans and winning games. But the truth is, you owe it to yourself to be a French. To be the kind of person who gives the young ABs in the team opportunities to prove their mettle.

Everyone talks about the genius of A.B. de Villiers. But spare a thought for French too. He made a difference. He gave talent an opportunity.

You should too.

For every rising star in the world, there are several others who unfortunately never get a chance to prove their worth. Equally talented, as capable but deprived of the opportunity. Success is about talent. *And* about opportunity. When talent meets opportunity, history gets made. Give young talent an opportunity.

GOOD ADVICE

Someone once said there really are no big problems in life. Only small problems that remained unattended to.

And the truth is, nothing is too small. Or insignificant. Everything counts. Everything matters. It all adds up.

A proven way to build a mindset of excellence is to focus on getting the small things right. Make that a habit.

***Do the small things right.** Every day. Day after day.*

The Socks and the Shoes

John Wooden is often regarded as the greatest coach. Ever. He was a basketball player and, in his early years, an English teacher too. And then went on to become the head coach at the University of California, Los Angeles (UCLA). He enjoyed tremendous success there, as UCLA won championship after championship. Several NBA superstars credit their success to the initial training under Coach Wooden.

As a basketball coach, Wooden did not see his role as merely grooming good basketball players. He saw his role as helping young people become good human beings. His focus was not only on athleticism and ball-handling skills. What mattered to him were old-fashioned values, like friendship, cooperation, enthusiasm and loyalty.

John Wooden was awarded the prestigious Presidential Medal of Freedom in 2003. And here's what President George W. Bush said while presenting the award:

> All his players will tell you, the most important man on their team was not on the court. He was the man who taught generations of basketball players the fundamentals of hard work and discipline, patience and teamwork. Coach Wooden remains a part of their lives as a teacher of the game, and as an example of what a good man should be.

There are several stories about what made Wooden a legend. My favourite story about him concerns his first coaching session with a team. Every year, a fresh batch of college kids would come in all excited for their first coaching session. They would be proud of having made it to the college team. There would be excitement in the air. And guess what would happen next?

In the first coaching session, John Wooden would focus on teaching players how to put on their socks and shoes. Yes, you read that right. These were all grown-up men all right. But the coach would start off by showing them how to put on a pair of socks—without wrinkles in the soles or near the toes. His logic was simple. If you are not careful, you might have a wrinkle in your socks. The wrinkle might get you a blister. The blister could slow you down. And that might cause you to miss a game. If you were any good, that might mean your team might lose a game they could have won. And the coach might get fired! Since those weren't desirable outcomes, he would want all his players to pay attention to how they wear their socks and tie their shoelaces. The message was simple. And direct. No wrinkles please!

The bigger message from that lesson was hard to miss: Success depends on small things. Often, what separates winners from losers are small, tiny differences. That little attention to detail can go a long way. Doing small things right, day after day, makes a big difference.

If you follow cricket and are a fan of the T20 format, you would have noticed there isn't much separating one team from another. On a given day, any team can win. But the team that will win more often, more consistently, is the one that will do the small things right. The team that, for instance, makes sure the bat is grounded when they are stealing a cheeky single. The one that shows the presence of mind to take an extra run. Or save one. In essence, the team that does the small things right. The one that makes sure there are no wrinkles in the socks.

As the coach of the UCLA team, John led them to ten championship wins over a period of twelve years, a record that hasn't come close to ever being broken. And while John spent time on skills and strategies, and on team culture and mindsets, it was his first lesson with each team that players would recall. With great fondness. It was a lesson that taught them the virtue of paying attention to details. Small things make a big difference. That's true for basketball. For cricket. And for the game of life too.

I sometimes think it is such a blessing for Indian cricket that the man in charge of young players is Rahul Dravid. The National Cricket Academy, the India Under-19 and India A teams are all under his watch. And knowing Rahul, you would sense there is a John Wooden behind 'The Wall'. He is someone who is focused on not just grooming good cricketers, but on helping groom good human beings. And I am wondering what Rahul Dravid's version of teaching players to wear their socks right is.

For the rest of us, it would be a good idea to make it a habit to do the small things right. Every day. Cross the cheques. Wear the seatbelt before you start the car. Kiss the spouse. Spellcheck emails. Open doors. Small things matter.

Not having a wrinkle in the socks can mean not having blisters on your feet. But that's not all. Not having a wrinkle in the socks can also mean having a trophy in your cabinet!

> Remember John Wooden's message. Pay attention to how you wear your socks and tie your shoelaces. No wrinkles please! The bigger lesson? Success depends on small things. Often, what separates winners from losers are small, tiny differences. That little attention to detail can go a long way. Doing small things right, day after day, makes a big difference.

The India–Australia cricket series of 2020–21 will be remembered as one of India's finest. What a fightback it was. Imagine losing the first Test match and being bowled out for 36, the team's lowest Test score ever. And then fighting back to win the next Test match. And then hanging in with grit and a prayer—to draw the third Test. And then pulling off an improbable win in the fourth Test to win the series. How did a team that had hit an all-time low bounce back?

R. Sridhar, the team's fielding coach, spoke about how Ravi Shastri, the head coach, told the team to wear that 36 like a badge. 'Wear it like a badge and you will be a great team,' he said. And we saw what happened.

Good idea to **use failure to spur yourself on to success**. Wear that badge. Learn your lessons. Failure can teach you plenty.

Never Forget the Lessons

Did you know that Facebook's headquarters in Palo Alto at one time belonged to Sun Microsystems?

Sun was one of the early giants of Silicon Valley—but died a silent death in 2009. When Facebook moved into the premises, they refurbished the entire place. But they didn't get rid of the Sun Microsystems signboard outside the office. They turned it over and put Facebook's sign in the front. The world outside sees the Facebook sign. While from the inside, the employees see the old Sun Microsystems sign. Why did they do that? Why didn't they just throw away the old signboard and get a new one?

Mark Zuckerberg, the co-founder and CEO of Facebook, provides the answers. He says he wanted the old sign to stay, to remind Facebook employees of what can happen if you take your eye off the ball. Like Sun Microsystems did. He wanted them to remember never to take their success—or even their existence—for granted. Interesting thought, isn't it?

Most of us look back at our past successes to inspire ourselves and motivate our teams. We showcase trophies won and retell tales of triumph to remind ourselves of what we need to do to win. We don't usually look at mistakes made, or at failures, to remind ourselves of what we ought not to do. Maybe we should. Every organization should ask the question, 'What's our equivalent of the Facebook/Sun signboard?'

Once, early in my career, I walked into the cabin of a shampoo brand manager. On the shelf in his room were samples of blockbuster products, some great packaging innovations, ad club award trophies and some eye-catching point-of-sale material too. No surprises there.

But what caught my eye was a leaky pack of anti-dandruff shampoo in a tall refill pouch. The blue shampoo had leaked a long time ago and smudged the outer pack. It wasn't one of those tiny sachets (that came much later) but a large pouch, almost like a bottle. 'What was this messy pack of half-leaked shampoo doing on the shelf?' I remember thinking. And the brand manager went on to tell me the story. He explained how the refill pack was one of the biggest launches he had been associated with. The pouch was a low-cost packaging option, an innovation that would allow the company to sell shampoo at lower prices. The project was fast-tracked to get the product in the market as soon as possible.

It was a mega launch. Sales teams and retailers were all impressed by the innovative packaging. And in the first three months, sales were well above target. Then disaster struck. The pouch began to leak. Complaints began to pour in. It turned out that over time, the shampoo was corroding the lining of the pouch, resulting in the leak.

The leak would mess up entire shelves at big stores. Shopkeepers were furious as other expensive cosmetics were getting damaged too. The product had to be recalled, trade had to be compensated, and the marketing team had egg (and some shampoo) on their faces.

'That pack there,' said the brand manager, 'is a reminder. For me and my team. A reminder that while we need to innovate, we also need to be careful. We need to test every element and not look for short cuts in the quest for speed.' Needless to say, he went on to have a successful career in the years ahead.

If I now told you that Howard Schultz, the CEO of Starbucks, has a bottle of Mazagran on his table, you would know why. Mazagran is a carbonated coffee drink that Starbucks launched in the '90s. And yes, you guessed right, it bombed. No one remembers the brand. But Schultz wants to make sure the lessons are not forgotten. That bottle has pride of place on Schultz's desk.

What's your Mazagran then? What's your leaking shampoo story? What's behind your company's signboard? Whatever your past mistakes, make sure they are not swept under the carpet. Make sure they are not forgotten. The lessons from those mistakes could hold the keys to your future success.

Tell those stories. Let your team know. Make sure there are reminders of those mistakes for all to see. Lest they forget.

Remember the words of George Santayana. 'Those who cannot remember the past are condemned to repeat it.'

Most of us look back at our past successes to inspire ourselves and motivate our teams. We showcase trophies won and retell tales of triumph, to remind ourselves of what we need to do to win. We don't usually look at mistakes made, or at failures, to remind ourselves of what we ought not to do. Maybe we should.

Martin Luther King, Jr, could have spoken about his masterplan for racial equality and put forth several arguments to highlight the injustice of discrimination. And no one might have remembered. Or cared. Instead, he said, 'I have a dream . . .' And the world listened, and it was changed forever.

In his Gettysburg address, Abraham Lincoln could have spoken about the damage caused by the Civil War and the need for a more people-oriented governing style. And what did he say? He talked about a government 'of the people, by the people, for the people'. And suddenly the whole world seemed to get it.

Great leaders recognize it's not only about what you say, but also about how you say it. The difference between a message that doesn't register and one that seems to stay forever is often in the way it is told. Find words, or a turn of phrase, that make your message stick. **Make it memorable.** *Think about it, and you will find why you still recall advice that a boss gave you many years ago. You do?*

I sure do.

Why Keep a Dog and . . .

The year was 1986. As I graduated from business school, I was delighted to have landed a job at Hindustan Lever Limited (HLL). HLL, which is now called HUL (Hindustan Unilever Limited), was, and still is, one of India's most respected companies. It was widely regarded as a fabulous training ground for sales and marketing professionals.

The typical career path for a management trainee in marketing was this. Spend the first three years in sales. Do the hard yards. Understand how sales and distribution systems actually work. And once you were done with that, you would get the privilege of becoming a brand manager, a marketing person. While doing the sales stint, you sometimes viewed it as the price to be paid to get to be a brand manager. And it was only later in life that you realized how valuable it was. That sales stint had a huge impact on your understanding of the business, and it helped you do a good job in later roles.

Becoming a brand manager was one of the several dream-come-true moments at HLL. Life was good. You now had the opportunity to do more 'thinking' work. You moved to the sexier, more glamorous head office. And you got to interact with those creative ad agency folks you had only heard about until then. All of which made the new role a heady cocktail of excitement, action, responsibility and fun. A few months into the role and I was having a great time. And I had learnt a valuable lesson too. A lesson I haven't forgotten.

Being a brand manager was exciting. Not only were you responsible for a brand's sales and profits, but you also got to create what you hoped would be some fabulous, memorable advertising. We all tend to think of ourselves as full of great ideas and super creative. For me, as a rookie brand manager, it was even more so. So it was not unusual for me to suggest changes in the creative work that the agency presented. Change the background a bit? The green needs to be darker, don't you think? And why don't we change the copy a bit? While it's a good idea, here's an even better idea. And so on. You get the drift, right?

After one such meeting, the boss called me into his office. And he gave me some advice. He said as a brand manager, my role in creating advertising was to write a powerful brief. It was to put together the data, the context, the marketing challenge and the task at hand. And then leave it to the agency to come up with the creative. 'Don't try and create the ad,' he said. 'That's not your job. Leave it to the experts.' And then he said something that still rings in my ears: 'Why keep a dog and bark yourself?'

That piece of advice, I'd like to believe, made me a better brand manager. No, it made me a better manager.

I stopped trying to tell the creatives how to do their jobs. My focus was writing better briefs, spelling out what I wanted and then leaving the rest to them. It might have been so only in my mind, but I could feel my relationship with the agency getting better. We both seemed to be viewing each other with greater, new-found respect.

I have sometimes looked back and wondered: What makes us behave like this? Why do we do this so often? Why do we keep a dog and bark ourselves? I figured there may be three reasons why we do this.

One, we overestimate our own abilities. Two, we assume a power situation—a relationship where the more powerful person decides how it should be done. We assume the person who is paying for the service is more powerful. And three, we have a poor opinion of other people's skills and abilities. We focus on what they do wrong rather than on what they are doing right.

Over the years, I have found the advice to be invaluable. Not only with ad agency folks but with all the people I have worked with. The lesson is simple. Let people do what they are good at. Don't tell the experts what to do. As a leader, be the person who sets the agenda (focus on the brief!) and let people do their jobs. Resist the urge to tell other people how to do their jobs.

And the line—'Why keep a dog and bark yourself?'—comes back to me often. In the unlikeliest of places. At fancy restaurants, for instance. The place may be rated high for its food and may even boast a celebrity chef.

But what do we do? We still want to tell the chef to add a little extra spice in the curry. Or tell him that he should make it tangier. We tell him—an aspiring Michelin chef—how he should make that dish.

Telling people how to do their jobs is a double whammy. One, you don't leverage their skills to the fullest. And two, they don't take ownership for outcomes. If it turns out wrong, too bad. You asked for it.

Empowerment and delegation are words leaders love to throw around. But the temptation to interfere and direct is hard to resist. Particularly in a world where the leader thinks he is the know-it-all.

Steve Jobs knew this too. He said, 'It doesn't make sense to hire smart people and tell them what to do; we hire smart people so they can tell us what to do.' As leaders, we all take pride in hiring smart people. And then we make the mistake—of telling them what to do.

Have you noticed what happens when you get into a cab in a city you are visiting? You lived there some years ago. The streets are somewhat familiar. You tell the driver where you want to go. And then what happens? You follow that up with 'Which route are you taking?', right? Rather than leaving it to the driver to decide the route, you overrule his view and tell him which road to take.

And then, as you crawl through the traffic and get late for the meeting, the driver has this 'I told you so' smirk on his face. Your problem, sir. You chose this route.

All this also raises your anxiety levels. You are responsible. You have the weight of the world on your shoulders. There's so much to do. You find yourself wasting time telling everyone else how to do their jobs. Instead of focusing on your own work and doing what only you can do best. Result? Unhappy colleagues. Under-leveraged team resources. Lack of ownership. Ineffective, stressed-out leaders. And lousy, lousy results.

Next time you are trying to get some work done, remember that piece of timeless advice: Leave it to the experts. Tell them what you need. And then get out of their way.

Why keep a dog and bark yourself?

> Let people do what they are good at. Don't tell the experts what to do. Resist the urge to tell other people how to do their jobs. Tell them what you need. And then get out of their way.

I remember a little incident from school. Every time there was a break, or a teacher was absent, there would be a lot of noise in the classroom. Everyone seemed to be talking, and then shouting to be heard until the noise reached a crescendo. And then the supervisor would walk in and sternly admonish the class with her trademark line, 'Is this a classroom or a fish market?' Ah, fish market! The place where everyone seems to be talking—and no one is listening!

Every time I see people arguing, or struggling to find common ground, I am reminded of the fish market. I worry that most conflicts arise because everyone is talking, and no one is listening. People start to shout louder to be heard, but no one is listening. No one is trying to understand.

It's a good idea to **listen rather than shout**. *You will suddenly find less conflict and more agreement.*

Life isn't a fish market after all.

How to Resolve a Conflict

There are two simple rules I learnt several years ago that have stayed with me. And they have made a bit of difference. One rule came from my English teacher. And the other from my father.

The first is the rule that taught me how to spell all those words that have an 'i' and an 'e' together. Which goes first? The 'i' or the 'e'? I am talking of words like belief, and foreign and receive. You might have learnt the rule too: '"i" before "e" when the sound is "ee", but not after "c".' Remember this simple rule, and you will never spell those words wrong again.

The second rule is the one that has helped me work better with other people. And helped me make better decisions. It has helped me get my point of view across, and appreciate conflicting viewpoints. At work and in life too. And that rule is 'U before C'. Understand before Convincing.

Remember the rule. When you are sure you are right and the other person is wrong, U before C. When you are convinced what the next step should be and a colleague disagrees . . . When you and your wife have a difference of opinion on what that teenager at home should do next . . . Remember that rule. U before C. Understand the other person's point of view before trying to convince them you are right. Look around. You will see acrimonious debates. And hardened positions that people are taking all around us. You will see smart, intelligent leaders taking calls without listening to dissenting voices. We can all benefit from the 'U before C' rule.

Imagine you are trying to hire a candidate. You think it should be candidate A. Your team thinks it should be B. So what do you do? You rattle off a list of compelling reasons why you think A is the better choice. Your colleagues try and talk about the merits of B. And you listen with a view to seeing if you can point out the flaw in their arguments.

The right decision might still be A. But you'd be better off if you first understood the team's concerns. Why do they think B is a better candidate? Do that and you will begin to see aspects of the candidates that you may have overlooked.

The icing on the cake? They, too, become more receptive to understanding your point of view. Because you've heard the conflicting voices and tried to understand them. Both sides begin to approach the decision with the aim of finding out what's right—rather than who's right. And there's much greater buy-in for the decision, even if there was a disagreement to start with.

Faced with a disagreement, we get busy trying to convince other people about how we are right. In a team setting, we flock together with the supporters, the folks who agree with us. And we isolate the voices that disagree. They become the 'bad guys'. The misfits. The guys who don't get it. And our tone and our body language make them feel like they are not a part of the team. We focus on and talk about all the evidence that supports our decision. And we ignore and dismiss the evidence that doesn't support our thinking.

One more thing. As a leader, even if you have made up your mind, and are convinced about what you need to do, hold the thought. Good leaders speak last. Don't be in a hurry to put your view out there upfront. That puts pressure on your team. Pressure to fall in line, to agree with the boss. The easy thing for everyone to say then is that the boss is right. 'Why waste time? Let's move on. He won't listen anyway.'

If you want to leverage the power of your team, listen. Understand. And then take a decision and convince other people. See the difference it makes, in terms of the quality of your decision-making, and the quality of your interpersonal relationships.

A quick glance at the WhatsApp messages you get will show you how people have forgotten to spell correctly. Most of them have forgotten the 'i' before 'e' rule. But you could argue that's not a big deal. What's sad, though, is when you see people trying to convince you they are right and you are wrong. When they hammer their views on you and expect you to agree, without trying to understand a different viewpoint. You want to remind them of that other rule, U before C, always.

'U before C' might be the secret to becoming a better leader, a better team player and a better citizen too.

Give yourself the 'U before C' edge. Understand before you convince. Always.

> Remember that rule: U before C. Understand the other person's point of view before trying to convince them. It is the secret to becoming a better leader, a better team player and a better citizen too.

Someone's unhappy, feeling lousy about herself and asks you what she should do to be happier. You tell her to be positive. And she says that's not easy.

A friend wants to lose weight and get fitter. And you tell them to work out and to go off carbs and sugar completely. And they tell you, 'That's not easy.'

It makes you think. We all want results. Success. Glory. But we want to do what's easy. Success is about doing the tough bits, the hard yards. You can do the easy stuff—and feel like you are busy, like you are doing a lot. But that's not what you were meant to be doing.

Don't get busy ticking off the C-category items on your to-do list and feel good. You need to do the big important tasks.

***Focus on what you need to do**, not on what's easy, not on what you like doing.*

The Lion and the Antelope

You've probably seen it before. A video of a lion going for the kill. The hushed, lazy move as it spots an antelope in the distance. The nervous look on the antelope's face as it senses danger. The fast-paced chase. The suspense: Would the lion win or would the antelope get away? And then finally, the kill. It's fascinating. The lion-and-antelope encounter plays out every day around the world. But behind it is an interesting insight, first shared by Newt Gingrich, former speaker in the US House of Representatives.

'A lion,' explained Gingrich, 'is fully capable of capturing, killing and eating a field mouse. But it turns out that the energy required to do so exceeds the caloric content of the mouse itself. So a lion that spent its day hunting and eating field mice would slowly starve to death. A lion can't live on field mice. A lion needs antelope. Antelopes are big animals. They take more speed and strength to capture and kill. And once killed, they provide a feast for the lion and her pride. So ask yourself at the end of the day, "Did I spend today chasing mice or hunting antelope?"'

That's a terrific question. So what's keeping you busy? Have you been chasing mice or hunting antelope? What's true for lions is true for us and our teams too. We focus on the easy stuff and simple tasks, instead of going after the more challenging pursuits that would stretch us and force us to give our best. Pursuits that give us the big rewards. Why does it happen that we all end up making the mistake of chasing mice instead of focusing on the antelope?

First, mice are easier to catch. Second, catching mice makes us feel that we are busy all day. And third, when we embark on the journey of catching mice, we get a feeling that success is assured, unlike the pursuit of an antelope, which could often result in failure. We don't like to be seen to be failing.

So we do what's convenient rather than what's needed. Before embarking on a new initiative, good leaders don't pose the question, 'Can we do it?' They ask the tougher question: 'Should we be doing it?'

Businesses and teams begin to win when they turn their attention to the most important task at hand. They know it won't be easy. But they also know it needs to be done. When everyone focuses on the big wins, there is a sense of excitement in the team. Everyone knows that to be successful, they all need to stretch every muscle and give their best.

Do you find that in spite of doing all you can, the rewards aren't coming your way? You need to pause and check: Are you chasing mice instead of the antelope? Lions recognize they weren't granted all that power to feed on mice. Likewise, individuals and organizations need to focus on the highest goals—the goals they were meant to achieve.

Michaelangelo got it right when he said, 'The greatest danger for most of us is not that our aim is too high and we miss it, but that it is too low and we reach it.'

Time, then, to send a reminder to yourself and your team. Forget the mice. Focus on the antelope.

> Are you chasing mice instead of the antelope? Are you doing what's convenient rather than what's needed? Before embarking on a new initiative, good leaders don't pose the question, 'Can we do it?' They ask the tougher question: 'Should we be doing it?'

We are born competitors. And we love it. We grow up competing. For admission into nursery school. For an extra mark that will help us make the cut-off for admission into engineering college. For a seat in a bus. The idea of winning and making other people lose becomes second nature.

Then we get to work and discover that the rules of the game are different. We continue to compete. But what might help us win is not competing but collaborating.

Time to hit the reset button. Think win-win. ***Stop competing. Start collaborating.***

The Fight for Oranges

It's a simple game that kids sometimes play at birthday parties. It's also a game that's become a simulation exercise in business schools around the world. The game goes something like this.

You have two teams and one sackful of oranges. The teams are briefed separately by the professor—or the parent—on the rules and objectives of the game. Once that is done, both teams figure that the task is straightforward. They need to get as many of those oranges as they can. The teams get to work immediately. They jostle and fight to grab the oranges, and in the process, some oranges get squished. They hoodwink each other, bribing, even pleading to get more oranges. And when all that seems to be of no avail, they arrive at a compromise. A 'win-win' settlement. They agree to share the oranges equally. Once that's done, the parent hosting the party, or the professor in class, steps in.

She asks the teams to say why they wanted the oranges. Both teams recall what was told to them at the start of the exercise. 'To make some juice out of the oranges,' comes the response from Team One. 'We wanted the oranges because we needed the peels to make some cake,' says Team Two. And the penny drops.

The reality dawns on both teams. They realize what might have been. If only they had spoken to each other and understood each other's needs, they both could have had all the oranges—and not just the half they ended up with. If only they had spoken to each other.

It happens to us all the time. We are all fighting to get as many oranges as we can. In our lives, we often find ourselves in a negotiation situation. And we get obsessed with 'getting what we want'. We seldom pay attention to what the other side might want. Good idea, then, to talk and understand the other person's point of view. What do they want? Why do they want it? Understanding that can pave the way for a better solution.

We all have a choice. We could either wear our competitor hat, or we could wear our collaborator hat. Most times, we lead our lives assuming we only have the competitor hat. We want to win. We want our way. And to hell with the other guy. Put yourselves in the other person's shoes. Communicate. Tell them why you want whatever it is that you are asking for. Chances are you will find a solution akin to the orange-and-peel game. Remember, in your wardrobe is a lesser-used hat, waiting for you. The collaborator hat. Wear it.

It's also good to remember that agreeing to a quick compromise (let's go 50:50!) isn't a win-win outcome. True, the two teams fighting for the oranges agreed to go half and half on that sack of oranges. But in reality, as both sides realized later, they could have both got the entire sack of oranges. A true win-win is not a compromise. A win-win occurs when neither side can get more without the other side losing something.

That, then, is the tale of the orange-and-peel game. A story that was shared by Roger Fisher and William Ury in their book *Getting to Yes*. It is a classic on negotiation, published almost four decades ago. The book might seem dated but not the principles and lessons it contains.

Think about it. Next time you are sitting on the negotiation table, or even trying to settle an argument with the spouse, remember the oranges.

And think of the peel too.

A true win-win is not a compromise. A win-win occurs when neither side can get more without the other side losing something.

BETTER DECISIONS

In our quest for answers, we all ask questions. Lots of questions. Learning to ask the right questions is a good first step to finding the right answers. A good example of that is how the lines between intent and action get blurred. We ask 'What would you do?'—and pat comes the right answer. Everyone knows what they should be doing. So the answer to 'What would you do?' is spot on.

And it's misleading.

The right question to ask is, 'What did you do?' Intent is nice. But action gives you the true picture.

Good idea, then, to remember to ***ask the right questions****.*

Cleaning the Wardrobe!

It's become a bit of a ritual in my life now. A once-in-a-couple-of-years kind of thing. My wife and I get into spring-cleaning mode and get down to emptying out stuff we don't need from our wardrobes. The intent is noble. It allows us to give away clothes we don't need, to people who might delight in wearing them. But the outcomes I have discovered are very different for my wife and for me. Something interesting seems to happen, every time.

I have a lot of fun cleaning my wardrobe. I find a pink shirt I had bought with great excitement but have never worn. I try it on and in the comfort of my bedroom, the pink shirt looks great. I resolve I must wear it sometime soon—it looks so cool! I chance upon a pair of corduroy jeans—an old favourite—and wonder how it had gone missing for the past year! I discover a shirt that was a gift, the tags still intact. It's a size too small, has always been, but I tell myself that my new-found love for the gym will ensure I fit into that shirt. Soon. And this seems to go on for a while. End result? I find I haven't done a particularly good job of throwing out stuff I don't need!

My wife goes about it very differently. She first sets aside the silk sarees and some once-in-a-lifetime clothes. These are in the safe zone, straight off the bat. She then attacks the rest of her wardrobe with a simple question: Have I worn this in the last twelve months? If the answer is yes, it stays; if the answer is no, it goes. Simple. Her logic is straightforward. If she hasn't worn it in the past year, she doesn't really need it. End result? The wife seems to achieve her objective and gets rid of clothes she doesn't need, while I find a few more clothes I haven't worn but must wear in the future.

As I thought of the difference in our respective approaches, it struck me that maybe there is a lesson in it for us all. The right question to ask in many situations in life is not 'What *would* you do?' It is, 'What *did* you do?' The right way to clean the cupboard is to ask, 'Have I worn it in the last twelve months?' And not, 'Will I wear it in the next twelve months?' Intent is a funny thing. It's enticing. It tricks us. Actions are the real deal.

And it's not only about the wardrobe. We don't like to let go, no matter what it is. Try telling a team leader that his team is overstaffed, that you can see that at least three people are surplus. And see how he reverts with the critical work he has in mind for those three people. Or imagine your wife pulls out that used-only-once vacuum cleaner from the attic. The packing is intact. And she is planning to give it away. See how your heart sinks, and you promise to spend Sundays cleaning the house. For good measure, you also tell her that the vacuum cleaner can also be used to clean the car.

So next time you are interviewing a candidate for a role, refrain from asking 'What would you do' questions. Instead, ask 'What did you do' type of questions. Don't ask, 'How would you deal with an underperforming subordinate?' Better to go with, 'Tell me about a time when you had an underperforming subordinate. What did you do?' Actions are far better indicators of ability and character than intent.

When evaluating candidates for a promotion, we sometimes get swayed by potential. Great pedigree. Suave communicator. And we downplay performance. Big mistake. We end up promoting people who say all the right things and then wonder why the promotion didn't quite work out as planned!

As a leader, you are probably very good at articulating your vision and strategy for the business. But wait, don't be in a hurry to go from one town hall to the next, to share all that you plan to do over the next five years. Take a minute to ask yourself the question: What have I done in the last month—or three—to make that vision come true? Talk about that. Talk about what you have done. Not what you plan to do. Actions trump intent. Always.

Time, then, for me to go back to my wardrobe for a second shot at spring cleaning!

> The right question to ask in many situations in life is not 'What *would* you do?' It is, 'What *did* you do?' Intent is a funny thing. It's enticing. It tricks us. Actions are the real deal.

It is often said that our lives are the cumulative result of the decisions we take. So how can we take better decisions?

For a start, beware of survivorship bias.

In evaluating data, look for the full picture. Don't get swayed by a biased sample of success stories. Look at the failures too. And suddenly, the picture will look different.

And remember, it's not only leaders who make decisions. We all make decisions that affect our lives, our outcomes.

Pause, think. And learn to ***make better decisions****.*

College Dropouts and Bomber Planes

Abraham Wald was an unlikely war hero. Unlikely because Wald wasn't a soldier or a general. He was a mathematician, a man who used maths to help save lives and win wars. Wald was a part of an outfit called the Statistical Research Group. The US armed forces often turned to the group for help and advice. And maybe we, too, should all turn to Wald for a valuable lesson in decision-making.

One of the problems the US Air Force was grappling with during World War II had to do with bomber aircraft. Too many of them were getting shot down. And the high mortality rate of those aircraft had the authorities worried. Each time a bomber made its way into enemy territory, there was a high probability that it would get shot down, and that the plane and the pilot would never return. What could they do to save them?

Adding extra protection to the aircraft's body seemed like an option. But making them strong, like battle tanks, was not likely to work. It would have made them so heavy that the planes would have struggled to take off in the first place. So, strengthening parts of the plane, and not the entire plane, appeared to be the solution. But which parts should they strengthen?

To help answer that question, they looked at all their bullet-riddled planes and mapped out exactly where the bullet holes were. They found that the bullets tended to be concentrated in three places: on the wings, at the centre of the body and on the tail. Wings. Body. Tail. The answer seemed to be staring them in the face. The commanders decided to put extra protection in those three areas. Problem solved!

Well, not quite. Enter Abraham Wald. He looked at the same bullet-distribution data and said that putting extra armour where most of the bullet holes were would be the wrong thing to do. Instead, he suggested they put extra protection on the parts where there were *no* bullet holes. Yes, you read that right. He advised them to reinforce the parts of the plane where there were no bullet marks. Why?

He reasoned that despite being hit by bullets in those places, the planes had made it back. They had to worry about the missing planes—the ones that didn't make it back. They were the ones that got shot in the places where there were no bullet holes—and could not make it back to safety. The places where there were no bullet marks were exactly the places where the planes were most vulnerable. And so, the planes that didn't make it back must have got shot there!

Wald's insights and inputs helped make the planes a lot safer and saved many lives too. Wald's analysis came to be referred to as 'survivorship bias', a phrase that refers to the logical error of concentrating on the people or things that made it past some selection process while overlooking those that did not, typically because of lack of visibility. In this case, they were looking only at the planes that had made it back, ignoring the ones that got shot down and never returned to base.

Survivorship bias is all around us. Young, ambitious men hear about heroes in Silicon Valley who dropped out of college, and they start to think that the secret to success in life is to drop out of college. It becomes easy to believe that college does not add much to our development and success. But this kind of thinking ignores the stories of those people who dropped out of college and ended up as underachievers, people who wasted their lives and never made it. We tend to ignore what the author Nassim Nicholas Taleb calls the 'silent evidence'.

It's a trap—a bias—that we all need to guard against. We do customer surveys, where we ask our customers what we should be doing to serve them better. But we ignore the non-buyers and the lapsed customers. Employee engagement surveys tell us what our employees think of the organization and what leaders should be doing to make the organization a great place to work. But we don't survey ex-employees! We don't ask them what made them leave. We all hail the stock-market guru who makes those three multibagger predictions, but we ignore the several dud predictions he had made over the years. And please, please watch out for those people who start off by telling you they slept on the streets and then tell you how they went on to become billionaires, so you can too. Several of their fellow street-sleepers are still there. On the street, that is.

So next time you are looking at data and making a decision, pause. And think of those bullet-riddled planes. Do that, and you might just avoid survivorship bias. Don't draw your conclusions looking only at the ones who made it. Look at the misses, the failures too.

As you will discover, the answers are seldom as obvious as they seem!

> Watch out for survivorship bias. Don't make the mistake of focusing on the successes and ignoring the failures. Don't just concentrate on the people or things who made it past some selection process while overlooking those who did not, just because you don't see or hear about the latter. Remember, the aircraft body needed reinforcement not where the bullet holes were—but where there were no bullet holes.

Business often resembles a game of chess. There's an enemy, there are armies. There's strategy, and attack and defence. And even a small pawn can make a difference to the ultimate result. And there's more.

Whether you are playing a game of chess or leading a team, you need to think a few moves ahead. It's not enough to think, 'Wow, I have a great move here.' ***You've got to ask, 'What happens next?'*** *Having a mindset that thinks of consequences beyond the immediate, that thinks of the next move, and then the next, can help ensure you make the right decisions.*

On the chess board. And in life.

Getting Rid of the Cobras

It happened over a hundred years ago. But there's a lesson in it that's still relevant for us.

The story goes that around the turn of the nineteenth century, there was a problem in Delhi. There were a lot of cobras all around. Fear was setting in, and the British rulers came up with a plan to rid the city of the cobra menace. They announced a handsome cash reward for anyone who would kill a cobra. All that a person had to do was hand over the dead cobra to the authorities and claim the money.

Soon after, the city became safer as people started to kill the cobras and claim their rewards. The number of cobras began to drop. But something interesting happened. Some clever folks saw an opportunity to make money from the reward scheme. So they decided to raise cobras in their backyards. People began to have their own little cobra farms. One by one, they would kill a cobra, hand it in and claim their reward. The authorities were puzzled. On the one hand, the number of cobra sightings had dropped, while on the other, they were continuing to pay out huge sums of money as rewards for killing cobras. They decided to stop the reward scheme.

Guess what happened next? All those enterprising folks who were rearing cobras had no use for them any more. In the quiet of the night, they let the cobras loose, and Delhi now had more cobras than ever before. A scheme intended to bring down the number of cobras ended up having the opposite effect. Thus was born the phrase 'the cobra effect'.

The cobras have all gone from our streets now, but the cobra effect continues to make its presence felt in our decision-making. Even today. Faced with a problem, we are quick to take action that seems like a solution. But we don't always think through what the second-order effects could be. Result? The problem gets worse.

Like it happened with a head of HR I know. She was worried. Only 17 per cent of the employees had filled up the engagement survey forms, and there was only a week left. When global HR put out data on the progress across countries, she felt bad seeing India as a laggard.

Only a handful of people were responding every day. She knew she had to do something to turn the trickle into a flood. She sent out a passionate email, telling employees how the response level was abysmal and how, across the country, very few people had responded to the survey. She was hoping that the message might move people into action.

But guess what happened? Employees who had not responded to the survey saw the mail—and heaved a sigh of relief. They were delighted to discover that they were not the only ones who had not responded. They were in good company! Even the trickle stopped.

In a crisis, you will sometimes come up with a quick decision that may seem like a solution to the problem. Good idea to pause and ask yourself the question, 'And then what?' Look for the second-order effects. It will help ensure that your actions are not compounding the problem, let alone solving it.

Watch out for the cobra effect.

> Faced with a problem, we are quick to take action that seems like a solution. But we don't always think through what the second-order effects could be. Result? The problem gets worse. Watch out for the cobra effect.

Problem-solving is a prized skill. We would all like to hire that experienced and skilled manager who has been through the same challenges and can help solve our problems. We all love that advice from a health specialist that can cure us of our illness. Or that business consultant who will come and fix our broken processes.

As the recent pandemic has once again proved, we love to focus on the cure. Prevention doesn't seem as cool or as attractive an idea.

Grandma was right when she told you that ***prevention is better than cure****. It's better but it is far less attractive.*

We all love a crisis. Because a crisis throws up a hero. No one really cares about that diligent colleague who prevented a crisis.

Maybe we should, no?

Steering Wheels and Seatbelts

In the mid-twentieth century, the automobile industry was at a crossroads. It was a few decades since Henry Ford's Model T had been launched, in 1908. The Ford assembly-line production system was making cars more affordable. More popular too. And horse-drawn carriages were making way for automobiles.

But there was a problem. Over 40,000 people were dying every year in car accidents, and that was proving to be a barrier to sales as well as a matter of concern from the safety standpoint.

The experts at the Ford Motor Company looked at the data on accidents and figured what was causing the largest number of fatalities: It was the impact of the driver's head hitting the steering wheel or the windshield. So, a lot of Ford's money and effort went into making the windshields better and safer. Innovations helped make the glass stronger, and it would splinter in such a way that there were no sharp edges. A lot of work went into making the steering wheels softer—to cushion the impact. It made sense to add these safety features to the steering wheel and the windshield, given that drivers were being thrown forward and crashing their heads into them.

Around this time, Robert McNamara joined the Ford Motor Company. He was a Harvard Business School alumnus and a veteran of the US armed forces. McNamara figured that for Ford, reducing car accident fatalities had to be priority number one. As he reviewed the ongoing work on softer steering wheels and safer windshields, he had an idea. Instead of softening the blow, what if they could prevent it? What if they could prevent the head from hitting the steering wheel and the windshield?

And that led to an innovation: the introduction of the seatbelt in automobiles. It was an innovation that revolutionized car safety and has helped save millions of lives ever since. If car travel has become a whole lot safer today, you can thank McNamara for it. He looked at the same problem as everyone else. But he saw it differently. He thought about ways of preventing the head from hitting the steering wheel, instead of looking at the means of softening the blow. This change in perspective worked. And it led to Ford introducing seatbelts in their automobiles. McNamara also went on to become the first president of the Ford Motor Company from outside the Ford family.

Thinking 'seatbelt, not steering wheel' can revolutionize our lives too. Learn to dive deeper into the real problem, and work on prevention rather than cure. The McNamara mindset can help us solve problems in our lives too. Don't take the problem as a given. Don't assume that the task is damage control. Instead, look for ways to prevent the problem from occurring. The best course of action is not always a solution to the problem but a way of preventing the problem. Facing a problem you need to solve? Go back one step. See what causes the problem. Then try and see what you can do to prevent it.

Take golf for instance. Golfers hit the ball from a starting tee. They drive along a fairway and aim to land the ball on the green, with the least number of strokes. And then putt it into the hole. As you can see, it helps to land closer to the pin on the green, as short putts are easier than long ones. One amateur golfer asked Jack Nicklaus, the golfing legend, for advice on how he could get better at the long putts. Nicklaus's response? Land the ball closer to the pin on the green, son!

What happens when shopkeepers reduce their purchase of a company's products? The company starts to see a drop in their sales. What do companies do then? They look for ways to incentivize shopkeepers to buy more. Schemes, incentives, discounts, the works. Instead, they should be taking the McNamara approach. Understand why shopkeepers are buying less, and what could the company have done about that. They will figure they need to improve the product to make more consumers buy it. That's the better solution.

What happens when employees leave an organization for a higher-paying job? The temptation is to look at revising salaries. Pay people more and match what they may be getting elsewhere. Instead, companies should look at why employees are unhappy and what's prompting them to seek out other jobs.

The mistake we all make is focusing on softening the steering wheel rather than looking for a seatbelt.

Next time you or your team are working to solve a problem, make sure you are attacking the right problem. The quality of our answers depends on the questions. Take a step back. Dig deeper. And ask yourself the question: Instead of solving this problem, what could we have done to prevent it?

Think seatbelts. Not steering wheels!

> Thinking 'seatbelt, not steering' can revolutionize our lives too. Learn to dive deeper into the real problem. And work on prevention rather than cure. The best course of action is not always a solution to the problem but a way to prevent the problem. Facing a problem you need to solve? Go back one step. See what causes the problem. And try and see what you can do to prevent it.

INFLUENCE

Have you sometimes thought you were so smart that you could pull a fast one on someone else? Done that? And felt good? Maybe you shouldn't have.

People are smarter than we think and can easily see through our intentions. And it leaves you feeling lousy when you realize that someone tried to take you for a ride.

Don't do that. Being candid and respectful of other people helps you build trust. And trust begets trust.

***Respect other people's intelligence.** At all times. Even in the seemingly small, insignificant things. That's where trust is built. Or destroyed.*

Who Are You Kidding?

I am guessing it has happened to you before.

You get a call out of the blue from an old friend. Someone you were good friends with but haven't been in touch with lately. He asks about you and the family. He talks about how he misses those good old days and then says, 'We must catch up. You must call me when you are in town. Let's grab coffee. Or a drink. In fact, you must come home.' And you start to feel so good that he took the initiative to call and check on you, after all these years.

Then, before hanging up, he asks, 'Do you have Rahul's coordinates? Could you share his number please? Need to call him today for some help.' And you say sure, no problem, will WhatsApp the number right away.

As you put the phone down, you figure exactly why he called. It was for that number. The opening bits about 'how's the family, long time, must catch up' somehow begin to feel artificial. You hit the delete button in your head on all those lines, because by the end of the call, you've figured out why he called.

Have you been at the receiving end of such a call? Or do you find this conversation familiar because you were the one who made that call? Yes? Well, time then to change the sequence. Time to change the 'batting order'.

Next time you call or write to someone for a favour—ask right upfront. Get to the point. And once that is out of the way, get down to asking about his work, his family and about catching up. This way, the other person knows exactly why you called. And once that's done, he'll appreciate the time you are taking to talk about all the other things. He will be more willing to believe everything you say.

Why do most of us get the sequence wrong? You could put it down to an instinctive aversion to tackling the tough, bad bits. We worry we will come across as the 'calling-only-when-we-need-something' kind of people if we ask for a favour right away. So we try and pave the way with a few minutes of small talk and hope that the person will think that's the reason we have called. We fool ourselves into believing we are doing it to make it easier for the recipient. Truth is, we are doing it to make it easier for ourselves.

But you know what? Other people are smarter than we think. They understand.

This happens with feedback in the workplace too. We are uncomfortable giving hard feedback. We fear for the person's self-confidence. So we first lace it with some positive stuff—and then get to the point. How does the recipient feel? By the time you are done, he knows the intent of the conversation was the hard feedback. He thinks you said the other stuff just as a build-up. Perhaps you didn't mean it at all.

It pays to be upfront. It builds trust. Candour adds to your credibility. Respect the other person's intelligence. By delaying getting to the point, you won't achieve anything. People respect honesty. Like you do.

Remember the early years of limited-overs cricket? The objective was to score as many runs as possible in 50 overs. But the teams would play cautiously in the beginning, preserve wickets and then slog in the end. Sanath Jayasuriya and Romesh Kaluwitharana and Mark Greatbatch changed all that. They attacked from the first ball. Pinch hitters got promoted up the batting order. And limited-overs cricket was never the same again. Maybe there's a lesson there for us all.

Next time you are writing a mail or making a call or asking for something, get to the point fast. In fact, get to the point first. And then say the rest.

Try it. Change the batting order.

It pays to be upfront. Candour adds to your credibility. Respect the other person's intelligence. By delaying getting to the point, you won't achieve anything. People respect honesty. Like you do.

Benchmarking is a popular tool in business. It's often used to compare a company's costs—or processes or talent—with peer-group companies or best-in-class organizations. The idea, then, is to identify gaps and try and bridge them to get better.

But there's a slight problem there. If you are not careful, you can end up playing catch-up all the time. The aim seems to be to become as good as the other guy. You focus on your weaknesses and your inefficiencies, and work to set them right.

Maybe we should think differently. Our best chance of success comes from focusing on our strengths, rather than working on our weaknesses. Trying to improve across all dimensions we are deficient in, can make us struggle towards finally—and hopefully—becoming average.

But our shot at greatness is through finding our unique strengths—that one thing that marks us out as special—and then going to town with it. Our own USP.

So, ***what's your USP?*** *What will you be remembered for?*

What's Your Popsicle Hotline?

The Magic Castle Hotel in Los Angeles has none of the razzmatazz that you might associate with a hotel in the land of Hollywood. And yet, it is among the highest-rated hotels in LA on most travel sites. How come?

Turns out that people who have stayed there can't help but talk about one unique feature: the hotel's popsicle hotline. It's a little red telephone mounted on the wall near the swimming pool. You pick up the phone and ask for a popsicle, any flavour that you'd like to have. And in a jiffy, a butler arrives with a fancy tray and your favourite popsicle. All for free.

Kids love that. As do grown-ups. Everyone loves a free popsicle. You sometimes see little kids splashing in the pool, eyeing the butler and the popsicles, unaware of the popsicle hotline. And the other children are quick to tell them about it.

The Magic Castle Hotel might have remained unknown had it not been for the Heath brothers—Chip and Dan—who wrote about it in their book *The Power of Moments*. What influences our memories of people and places? As the Heath brothers see it, it is the powerful moments that have the greatest impact. Those standout moments matter more than the overall experience. And that explains why the Magic Castle Hotel is an experience to remember. It's not about the rooms and facilities, or the size of the pool. It is the popsicle hotline that makes it unforgettable.

Maybe we should all draw inspiration from the Magic Castle Hotel. We all need to create our own version of the popsicle hotline. Powerful, memorable knock-the-socks-off moments. Moments that make our friends and family, colleagues and customers, say, 'Wow! That is so cool!'

The Magic Castle Hotel could have spent a lot of money on, say, refurbishing the rooms, or making the lobby a little snazzier, or adding one more speciality restaurant. But most likely, none of those would have helped the hotel stand out. But the popsicle hotline? It creates moments of delight and memories that their guests cherish. And that makes all the difference.

The popsicle hotline reminded me of a time in my own career many years ago. I was the regional head and was out with my sales team on a market visit in Calcutta, when I got a call from the CEO's office. As you might imagine, when the CEO's assistant tells you the boss wants to speak with you, you begin to wonder what the problem might be.

But on that particular day, the CEO had something unusual to say. He wanted a favour. He wanted me to buy a saree, which he wanted to gift to a friend's wife. Could I please do that for him? The CEO was known to be a tough taskmaster, someone driven by principles and values. And a request like this one seemed strangely out of character. I said I wasn't very good at buying sarees. I tried to wriggle out of the task. And then I said something about doing it later, with a little help from my wife. But he would have none of it. He wanted it done right away. He indicated a price range and insisted that I go pick up a saree. And then he said, 'I want you to buy a nice saree, right away, and go home.' Then, after a pause, he added: 'Give it to your wife and tell her that her husband has been promoted!'

Wow. It happened several years ago but still makes my hair stand on end as I think of that moment. Like everyone else's career, mine too has had its ups and downs. Moments of joy and despair. But you can see how a few powerful moments help shape our memories of times gone by.

Time, then, for you to create your own moments. Make that anniversary dinner unforgettable. Send that customer a little something that melts his heart. Make that promotion announcement special.

Create your own popsicle hotline!

> Maybe we should all draw inspiration from the Magic Castle Hotel. We all need to create our own version of the popsicle hotline. Powerful, memorable moments that knock the socks off our teams. Moments that make our friends and family, colleagues and customers, say, 'Wow! That is so cool!'

How easy is it for you to ask for a favour? And how do you respond when someone asks you for a favour? How do you feel? Being able to ask for help is a master skill. And yet, we all hesitate to ask. Remember, if you ask, you may or may not get. But if you don't ask—you don't get.

A good way to get comfortable asking for favours is to become the kind of person who helps—when asked.

Ask for help.

Can You Do Me a Favour, Please?

I grew up in Delhi in the '70s, and some of my most vivid memories are of living through the 1971 Indo–Pak war. I remember the trenches in the Defence Colony market near our home, and the blaring sirens. I remember the mix of fear and excitement as I helped my brother cover the windows of our house with brown paper. And most of all, I remember the sorrow and agony of our neighbour, the aunty next door. She was the proud wife of a retired army man. And the proud mother of a young army officer who had gone missing in the war. I can still picture her sobbing and wailing.

I've always admired folks from the armed forces, even if only from a distance. And I believe there's a lot we can learn from them. Here's something I have learnt in recent times from a friend, a retired brigadier. He has changed the way I think, and the way I behave. But first, a flashback. And a confession.

I tended to have a very poor opinion of people who sought favours. As someone who took pride in fighting his own battles, I didn't believe in asking for favours.

Nor did I grant them. I believed we lived in a world where everything was earned, and no favours were sought or given. If someone requested me to speak to an HR head to help him land a job, I found it difficult to act on that request. If someone wanted me to ask a friend for a ticket to an IPL game or for a school admission for their kids, I would be reluctant to do that. Asking for favours wasn't easy for me. Must confess, I struggled with it.

And then, I met the Brigadier. Brigadier Tolani. We soon became dear friends, and golfing buddies too.

Two things struck me about him. One, he would ask for help. Often. And two, I noticed that he would do all he could to help other people. To get things done for others.

I would get a call from him, and he would ask if I knew someone in that large MNC. Why? Because they were sponsoring a golf tournament and while he had an invite, he wanted one for a friend. Or he would ask me for help with getting a summer internship for a friend's daughter. He wanted to help his friend. So, it would often happen that he would want me to call a friend and ask for a favour—for a friend of his or, worse, for a friend's friend. I'd struggle with that big time. And in most cases, I'd let it be and hope that he wouldn't follow up.

But he always would.

And, of course, I knew that if anyone—anyone at all—wanted help, the Brigadier was the man to turn to. Wanted your car serviced in a hurry? He'd call a friend and request for fast-track VIP service when you turned your car in. Wanted help with getting papers signed by a notary in a distant city? He'd call his contacts, find someone who could help and then move heaven and earth to make sure your job got done. An incredibly helpful man he was, the Brigadier.

And then, one day, I asked him how he could so easily ask for help. He smiled and gave me a look that seemed to say, 'Yeah, and I know how you struggle with that!' Then he said something that got me thinking. He said, for the better part of his life he had fought for the country, for the lives of people he didn't know. His life was all about helping others. 'Even today,' said the Brigadier, 'I would happily do all I can to help someone else. And since I would do that myself, I imagine other people would do the same for me too. I don't see why anyone wouldn't help me. So I ask! If you ask, you usually get. And yes, if someone asks me, I do all I can to make sure they get what they are looking for.'

I must confess, that conversation changed me. Today, if someone asks me for a favour, I try and help. I try my damned best. And now that I do that, I find it a little bit easier to ask for help too.

One of my all-time favourite books is *Influence* by Robert Cialdini. There's a little piece in there that's been stuck in my mind for a long time. It's about favours, and how we respond when someone thanks us for a favour we've done. Think about it. How do you respond?

Imagine you've taken pains to send your driver to the other end of town to deliver a parcel that a friend needs. She calls to say thank you. And you say, 'Oh, that's hardly anything. Don't even mention it.' Or you make up a story and say that the driver was going to be in that part of town anyway, no big deal. Sounds like you, right?

Cialdini says we get it wrong. The friend feels special and is delighted that we took the trouble to send the driver and the parcel all the way. But when we tell her, you are welcome, oh it's nothing, we are telling her, 'No, you are not special.' When we lie that the driver was going to be there anyway, we are telling her, 'Come on, I wouldn't send the driver that far. Not for you.' That, Cialdini informs us, is the wrong response.

When someone thanks you for a favour, here's what Cialdini suggests you should say: 'You are welcome. And I know you would do the same for me!' The chain of helping each other is set in motion.

Guess what? My world is a much better place now. Maybe that's how we were always meant to live. Helping each other. So thank you for the lesson, Brigadier.

And yes, while we are on the subject, tell me, how can I help?

> Remember the words of the Brigadier: 'I would happily do all I can to help someone else. And since I would do that, I imagine other people would do the same for me too. So I ask! If you ask, you usually get. And yes, if someone asks me—I do all I can to make sure they get what they are looking for.'

Life lessons are everywhere. Even on our streets. A memorable lesson I learnt several years ago had to do with the power of social proof.

We all want to belong. We want what other people have. We want to do as others do. So if you want to sell an idea, find a set of early adopters. The first set of followers, the first set of fans will help you get a hundred fans, then a million.

*But **enlist the early adopters first. Fast.***

The Salesmen of Churchgate

Okay, you've just turned entrepreneur. You have a fantastic product that solves a real customer problem. You are confident it will be a runaway success around the world. You are dreaming of yachts and limos, and unicorns and chalets in the south of France. Slight problem, though. The first customer is nowhere in sight. Sigh! What should you do?

Or perhaps you are a leader with a fantastic idea. You know it can be a game changer for your organization. You are dreaming of that congratulatory call from the CEO and that out-of-turn promotion. Slight problem, though. No one is buying your idea.

Well, here are lessons from a long time ago that you might find useful. These are good reminders of what it takes to sell an idea, or a product or service.

Flashback, then, to the '70s. School breaks are always memorable. And for me, the vacation in 1978 was particularly special. I had finished my ICSE exams in December 1977 and college, in Mumbai, was only scheduled to start in June next year. It was the most fun six months of my life!

I would take the local train every morning to the Churchgate station and spend the day watching cricket. I would walk across to the Cross Maidan, or farther on to the Azad Maidan, to watch cricket matches. Just being able to—nay, being allowed to—take a local train on my own seemed like a marker of my growing up. I wasn't a kid any more.

The Times Shield was on at that time. It was a popular interoffice tournament, featuring several Indian Test cricketers. And I can recall a young, still-in-college Sandeep Patil hitting huge sixes. I remember Padmakar Shivalkar, playing for Tata Electric, as you would expect an old faithful Tata employee to do. And I remember the buzz in a Nirlon game when their star opener (and my hero) arrived at the ground, in his shining new Premier Padmini. I even remember the car's registration number: 123. Yes, it was Sunil Gavaskar. It was a different era for cricket. But boy, was it fun.

Catching the local train. Watching cricket at Mumbai's maidans. Snacking on pav bhaji and vada pav. Skimming through and buying second-hand books on the footpaths near Flora Fountain. I guess those are the defining memories of the phase when I grew up from a schoolboy into a young man. It was also around that time that I learnt my first lesson in selling, a lesson I have not forgotten.

On the pavement outside the Churchgate station were an assortment of vendors. There were vendors selling cheap sunglasses. Railway pass covers. Vegetable peelers that I suspected worked only in the hands of the seller. And fabric for shirts and trousers.

There always seemed to be a crowd around the guy selling material for shirts and trousers. With time to kill, I would often stand there and watch. Fascinated. The prices seemed attractive, quite like the material. It was fun watching the men, old and young, jostling to pick their favourite designs from all those pieces laid out on the pavement. One man would point to a blue striped shirt piece in a corner, wanting to feel the fabric before buying it. Almost instinctively, someone else would want to see that exact same piece too. And one of those sales guys would toss the shirt to one of the customers, but only after pausing for a minute, as if to decide which of the two had hit the buzzer first.

There were two or three salesmen, and ten or fifteen customers. It was always crowded. Business was brisk. And you could see cash being handed out in exchange for a shirt piece or two. It often felt like people didn't want to miss out as they watched others around them buying. They didn't want to miss the party. For me, this was a complete 'time pass'. I would love to believe that it was the first sign of my interest in consumer behaviour and sales, but I doubt it. I was just admiring the spirit of enterprise of the typical Mumbaikar. Imagine selling fabric to commuters on the roadside to make a living, and, as the crowd at that place suggested, a pretty decent living too. I was convinced it was the crowd there that had attracted me and made me—and several others—want to take a look.

Then, one evening, I noticed something interesting as I watched the action. 'Weren't some of the men buying the fabric the same ones who had been there the previous day?' I wondered. They looked familiar. At least three or four of them. I wondered if they were 'regulars' like me, window-shopping. But no, I saw them picking up some pieces and paying cash for the same. Repeat buyers, perhaps? It got me thinking.

My doubts were confirmed when I stopped by at the same place the next day. And the next. The same set of 'customers' were there every time. There they were, pointing to that grey trouser piece in the far corner, wanting to see it up close. They were picking up more than one piece. Paying cash. Collecting the change. And the other people standing around seemed to be mimicking their behaviour. Those four guys, I figured, weren't customers. They were part of the sales team and were there every day. The group of six or seven shirt-sellers had well-defined roles. At any point in time, two or three of them were sellers and the others were buyers. Judging by the crowds they attracted, the ploy seemed to be working rather well. Business was booming.

Think about it. All those years ago, here was a group of people who had figured out an eternal truth about human behaviour. We find safety in numbers. We are comfortable taking action when we see other people doing the same thing. We like what other people like. We want what the other guy wants. If so many people are buying it, it must be good, we tell ourselves.

It's a lesson that has stayed with me, long after my tryst with the fabric-seller of Churchgate. It's not a lesson in sales. It's a life lesson. We all like to belong. We like to be a part of the tribe. And a good way to get people to take the leap and buy your product is to show them that other people are doing it as well. The same principle works when it comes to selling an idea. Find some early adopters to buy into your idea.

Even as a customer, I am often reminded of the shirt-seller of Churchgate. I want to watch the shows that other people are watching. I want to follow people on Twitter that other 'people like me' are following. I am scared of buying something on Amazon that looks very good but has no reviews. I think of those fake reviews on e-commerce sites. The paid likes and followers on social media. My mind flashes back, and I see a bunch of familiar faces standing around a street vendor, buying fabric for shirts and trousers all day long, day after day. That vendor outside the Churchgate station has vanished. But those salesmen-turned-customers haven't gone away. They have moved online!

I was telling a friend who works in the retail space about this. And he said he sees this phenomenon play out in retail stores every day. There may be a hundred television sets on display in a store. But if you want to generate interest and inquiries for a slow-moving model, put a 'sold out' sign on it, and watch the fun. Everyone wants that model. Everyone wants what everyone else wants.

Or if you are trying to sell cookies at a store, don't create a shelf that's choc-a-bloc with those packs. Create a half-filled, slightly haphazard display on the shelf. Make it appear like people have been taking away packs from the shelf. And watch the magic. People want to buy what other people have bought.

And then, my retailer friend told me about Humpty Dumpty and the shopping cart.

Humpty Dumpty was a supermarket chain in Oklahoma, United States, in the 1930s. Sylvan Goldman was the owner. He noticed that shoppers only bought as much as they could carry in their hand-held baskets. Once the basket was full, or too heavy, they headed to the checkout. As the shop owner, he wanted them to buy more. And he knew they would if he could solve the problem of the overloaded hand-held basket. Thus was born the idea of the shopping cart.

Goldman designed and manufactured a 'shopping basket with wheels'. He then arranged for a large number of those carts to be available outside the store. He even ran ads telling customers that they no longer needed to carry heavy baskets at Humpty Dumpty. He knew he had a winner—a unique service that addressed a real customer need in a simple way. And guess what happened?

The shopping cart was a flop. There were no takers. The young women didn't go for it because it seemed too much like pushing a baby in a pram. The men didn't want to look like sissies, so they too stayed away from the shopping cart. Disappointed, Goldman felt like giving up and pulling the carts out. But he didn't.

Instead, he hired young models, men and women. Their only job was to pick up the carts and move up and down the aisles, pretending they were shopping. It worked. Seeing them, other men and women began to use the carts too. The rest, as a visit to any modern-day supermarket will tell you, is history.

Critical to the success of any idea or initiative is the first follower. The first customers. The early adopters. Do whatever it takes to get them. And then see your idea take off.

Next time you find yourself struggling to sell your product, service or idea, pause. Think of the fabric seller in Churchgate. Or the first shopping cart. Find the first customer.

It's not about how good your idea is. It's about finding the first follower.

> We all like to belong. We like to be a part of the tribe. And a good way to get people to take the leap and buy your product is to show them that other people are doing it as well. The same principle works when it comes to selling an idea. Find some early adopters to buy into your idea.

Indeed the [illegible] young [illegible] men and women. There [illegible] and [illegible] worked. [illegible]

Critical to the success [illegible] is the [illegible].

Next time you [illegible] product [illegible] the first [illegible] the [illegible].

[illegible]

[illegible]

TEAMWORK AND CULTURE

Time is a precious commodity. Have you sometimes felt you don't have enough of it?

Good idea to figure out how you are spending your time. Most of us spend so much time on trivial things that we don't have time for what really matters.

It's not that you don't have enough time. It's that you have been spending it on the wrong things.

Reclaim your time, and reclaim your life. Make sure you spend your time doing the really important things in your life. It's your life. Get your priorities right.

And ***allocate your time wisely****.*

Everyone Loves the Bicycle Shed

Remember Parkinson's law? It says that 'work expands to fill the time available for its completion'. You've probably heard it before. And I am guessing we've all experienced it too, without even knowing it. The law owes its origin to C. Northcote Parkinson, a British historian and author.

Parkinson wrote this as the opening line of an essay in *The Economist* in 1955, and it has since become an oft-quoted management principle, a fact of life even. But there is another lesser-known law from Parkinson that we should all be aware of. One that's become even more significant in a world filled with back-to-back meetings and never-ending webinars. He wrote about it in 1957. But look at what happens in meetings and boardrooms today, and you will notice that nothing has changed.

Parkinson used a story to explain this law. It's the story of a committee that's meeting to discuss a three-point agenda. The first point concerns approval to sign a contract to build a $10 million reactor. The second point on the agenda is about building a bicycle shed for workmen that will cost

$350. And the third point concerns approval for a budget of $21 to provide refreshments to the Welfare Committee.

As the wise men and women take their seats in the meeting room, here's what happens. The $10 million dollar reactor contract gets approved in two and a half minutes, primarily because $10 million feels like a very large number that most people can't comprehend, and also because this reactor thing is too technical anyway. Everyone assumes that the folks concerned would have done their homework, since this is such a high-value decision. One man, who knows all about reactors, tries making a point, but he soon discovers it is of no use because no one else understands what he is saying. Nor do they seem to want to understand. And the $10 million reactor deal gets approved. In a jiffy.

Up next is the proposal for building the $350 bicycle shed. Now, everyone in the room is familiar with bicycles and bicycle sheds. The HR guy talks about the company's tradition of taking care of employees. The finance guy says that he cycles to work every day and leaves the bicycle out in the sun, and that there's never been a problem. He says he can't understand why we need a bike shed at all. The debate moves to the length of the shed and whether it should cater for current needs or for future requirements. Someone suggests that they should relook at the roofing material. Since aluminum is expensive, they should use asbestos instead. That could save $50. The debate moves to the colour of the roof. Grey or green?

This goes on for over an hour and finally, the bike shed gets approved. With an asbestos roof. Grey in colour.

And everyone is happy that the fruitful deliberations have helped save $50.

Then begins the discussion on the approval of $21 for refreshments. This is everyone's favourite. Everyone knows their tea and coffee. Everyone has a view. Tea or coffee is always an interesting debate, and this seems as good a time as any to rekindle that old debate. People talk about how it should be made, and where they should buy it. Some people, who may have been silent during the asbestos versus aluminum debate, feel here's their chance to speak up. After all, no one wants to leave such an important meeting without having spoken up and offered a viewpoint. After an hour and a half (that feels like three), the committee is close to approving the $21 for refreshments. But there are some suggestions and questions that need to be looked into. So it is agreed that a separate meeting will be convened in the following week, to make sure the additional data is available and the decision can be made. To approve the $21 budget.

Sounds familiar? See this happening at your meetings? It happens everywhere. More often than we like. And certainly more often than we would like to admit. Big issues are summarily dealt with because we don't want to take the trouble to understand them. And then everyone digs into the trivial issues. This came to be known as Parkinson's law of triviality. Or, as it is more popularly referred to, the bicycle-shed effect. The law states that the time an organization spends on discussing an issue is inversely proportional to the importance of that issue. We waste time on the trivial things we are comfortable with, rather than focusing on the more important stuff that we may not understand.

The bicycle-shed effect also refers to our irresistible urge to spend time discussing and debating silly little details, rather than the issue itself. So the focus shifts from whether or not we should have the bicycle shed to what the roof should be made of and whether it should be grey or green. The bicycle-shed effect might also explain why people often speak up at meetings. They do it not because they have a point to make but because they want to show they are familiar with the subject. It's almost like people feel they must speak up—or risk giving the impression that they have not contributed at all.

As leaders, it is good for us to be aware of the bicycle-shed effect. If you are in a meeting where people are discussing something you don't understand, listen in. Ask questions. Don't switch off or dismiss it as inconsequential. Make an effort to understand the issue as well as you can.

And be wary of the trap too. You might be debating the $21 decision forever, while letting slip the $10 million decision. Picture this: The wife asks if it worth paying an extra Rs 20,000 for the metallic-blue paint on the new car she wants you to buy her. You spend half an hour explaining how it makes no sense—that a car is a car, colours make no difference, this is a marketing gimmick. And though she so loves the metallic blue, she says she will go with what you say. You feel good that you've saved Rs 20,000. But you forget that you had not spent much time debating whether you should be buying the Rs 15 lakh car in the first place!

Good lessons to remember. And yes, next time you find someone wasting time discussing trivial things, press the pause button. Bring them back to the big issue.

And tell them about the bicycle-shed effect.

> Beware! The time an organization spends on discussing an issue is inversely proportional to the importance of that issue. We waste time on the trivial things we are comfortable with, rather than focusing on the more important stuff that we may not understand.

Building a fabulous team is one of the key challenges for a leader. Get the team right, and everything will start to fall into place.

And yet, several leaders get it wrong. They attract great talent but fail to build a great team. Maybe we can all learn a lesson from the leaders who got it right.

Build a star team. Not a team of stars.

This might make you wonder at first about what the difference might be between the two. But you'll soon figure it out. Focus on building a great team, not just pulling together great individuals. Do that, and watch the magic begin.

Team of Stars or Star Team?

Most successful organizations take pride in their ability to attract great talent. 'We only hire the brightest and the best,' an HR head said to me the other day. 'Don't they all say that?' I thought to myself. And if you've been responsible for hiring people for your organization, you would say the same thing too. We all look to hire the very best people we can find, and afford.

Maybe it's time to do a rethink.

The teams that win aren't always the ones that have the best talent or the brightest minds. These are the ones that have the right people in the right roles, across the spectrum. The ones who have teamwork working for them. Look around, and you'll see that it's not big-name talent that leads to success. It's something else.

Indian cricket's annual showpiece, the Indian Premier League (IPL) bears testimony to that too. There was a team that, for a while, boasted the three most explosive batsmen in the game. They had Virat Kohli, Chris Gayle and A.B. de Villiers. Did they ever win the championship? No. Because, as fans and experts will tell you, their bowling attack was so weak that no total seemed adequate. And then there were the Rajasthan Royals, the champion team of 2008. They were led by Shane Warne, the thirty-eight-year-old former great and an astute leader who was often referred to as the best man to have never captained Australia in Test cricket. And in almost every position, they had a specialist, albeit a not-so-well-known name. Their all-rounder was a nineteen-year-old rookie called Ravindra Jadeja. Opening the batting was Swapnil Asnodkar, an explosive, unknown hitter from Goa. And there was the big-hitting Yusuf Pathan from Baroda, whose younger brother was in fact the more famous India player. No big stars. And yet they finished on top.

There's a lesson in there for those of us looking to build a terrific team. Don't aim to build a team of stars. Focus instead on building a star team. A team wins not because it has the eleven best people playing, but because it has the best eleven. Think about it. As coaches and captains will often tell you, team balance is of prime importance. You often have to drop a star player and include a novice—to get the balance of the team right.

Hiring well, then, is not about getting the best talent to work for you; it's about getting the *right* talent in. And about leveraging the power of teamwork. How can you do that? Here are three pointers on hiring for success:

1. Good fit vs great guy

Before you hire, make sure you have a clear understanding of the role you are hiring for. Remember, what you are looking for is a person who fits the role, not a 'great guy'! We are all guilty of interviewing a person and concluding that she or he doesn't fit the role—but still wanting to hire them because they are a great talent. 'We'll find a role. Let's get them on board,' goes the refrain. Result? A lot of smart people join the team, with no clearly defined roles. Expectations are not spelt out. Reporting lines are blurred. Accountability is diluted. The newly hired great talent feels underutilized and undervalued, and eventually ends up becoming an underperformer—who quits. Having two outstanding batsmen who don't get to bat is not of much use if a half-decent wrist spinner is what the team needs in the game.

2. The right chemistry

Great teams are created not when you have star performers in each role but when they come together as one team to make magic. Do people enjoy working together, or do they merely tolerate each other? Good teams and great organizations are built when teammates respect each other and enjoy each other's company. Check for chemistry—before you hire! I know of the head of a private equity fund who has an interesting hiring process. Once she thinks she's got the right person for the role, she will get several of her colleagues to meet the candidate and spend time with him or her. Over dinners, lunches and shoot-the-breeze sessions, the team gets a good sense of whether they would enjoy working with the new hire. More importantly, the candidate too gets a feel for whether this is a bunch of people they would want to spend their working hours with. A clear win-win.

3. Eagles in formation

As PepsiCo began to build its India team some three decades ago, the brief was simple: Hire eagles who will fly in formation. The two seemingly conflicting ideas made that an interesting brief. In looking for eagles, they were looking for high-flyers all right. But the caveat—and the secret sauce—was that PepsiCo was looking for high-flyers who would be good team players too. When hiring, we focus too much on the individual and their skills, and too little on the team-player bit. Eagles who refuse to fly in formation might deliver in the short term. They are, after all, high-flyers. But soon, politics, rivalries, silos and turf wars become the norm. And performance suffers.

Focusing on building a team full of stars often means opening the doors to ego clashes. And to infighting and fiefdoms. The 'I' becomes bigger than the 'We'. And discord and dysfunctionality become defining characteristics of the team. There's also an added danger when you have too many intelligent people—or very talented people—in the same team. Each of them delegates the responsibility to someone else. No one takes ownership. No one in the team thinks too hard. Because everyone assumes someone else would have done the thinking anyway. This is the equivalent of a batsman throwing away his wicket thinking someone else will score the runs.

That's quite unlike what happens in a star team, where everyone is focused on creating a whole that is greater than the sum of the parts. In a star team, each member is clear about his or her role and is doing their damned best to help the team win.

Michael Jordan was right when he said, 'Talent wins games, but teamwork wins championships.'

A good lesson to remember. The best eleven trumps the eleven best. Any day.

> Don't aim to build a team of stars. Focus instead on building a star team. A team wins not because it has the eleven best people playing, but because it has the best eleven. Think about it.

If you are looking for a mantra that can help you figure out what you should be doing in any given situation, here it is. Just two words: ***It depends.***

Remember that, and you won't get fixated on ideas. You won't get stuck with thinking that if it worked in the past, it would work in the future too.

'It depends' will remind you that there is no one right answer. There is seldom 'one right way' to do things. As the saying goes, there are many ways to skin the cat.

And learning to know which way to choose starts with knowing that 'it depends'.

Strong Links and Weak Links

It was a Malcolm Gladwell podcast that got me thinking. Is the strength of a team determined by its weakest link? Or by its strongest link? Traditional wisdom would have us believe that a team is only as strong as its weakest link. So we all get busy fixing the weak link, covering the chinks. But Gladwell suggests we might have been getting it wrong. At least half the time.

The answer, it turns out, is 'It depends'. That's right. It depends.

Gladwell points out that in a sport like football, it is the weakest link that impacts your chances of success. A superstar striker might make a few brilliant plays but may or may not succeed in scoring every time. And a weak teammate might make a mistake that hands the ball to the opposition, resulting in a game-defining goal. Leicester City, who won the Premier League not so long ago—without any real stars—are a good case in point. So in football, it makes sense to strengthen your weak links.

Unlike say, in basketball where one star player could get control of the ball and do a slam dunk at the other end of the court, almost all by himself. One miss, one mistake doesn't hurt too much. LeBron James almost single-handedly took the Cleveland Cavaliers to the NBA final playoffs, with very little support from his teammates. How could he do it alone? Well, basketball is a strong-link sport. Unlike football.

As leaders, it might be useful for us to look at our own organizations and teams, and answer this question: Are we playing a weak-link sport or a strong-link one? The answer would help define our hiring strategy, as well as our training and development agenda. If you are an ad agency, it makes sense to hire—even at a high cost—a super-talented creative hotshot. She will create those amazing campaigns that will set the cash registers ringing. She will win you awards and bring glory to the agency. As opposed to, say, if you are in a business, trying to build a large customer service unit or a sales team. Having one superstar sales guy or a rockstar customer service associate may be nice. But it won't have as much impact as lifting the average and strengthening the weak links.

The strong link–weak link theory holds useful lessons for teams in the Indian Premier League too. How can they decide whether they should break the bank to get that marquee player to play for them? One way to look at it could be that when it comes to batsmen, T20 is a strong-link sport. One batsman can destroy the opposition, bat through the majority of the 20 overs and win you a game. So it makes sense to bid for that superstar big-hitting batsman. But when it comes to bowlers, it's a weak-link sport. No matter how good your star bowler is, he can only bowl 4 overs. And often games are lost because of the number of runs given away by the fifth bowler. So making sure your fifth bowler is not a terribly weak link can be the key to success.

Food for thought. As you watch the next football or IPL game, it would be a good idea to see how the strong link–weak link theory might apply to your favourite team.

And to your team at work too.

> Is the strength of a team determined by its weakest link? Or by its strongest link? It depends. The right question leaders must ask is: Are we playing a weak-link sport or a strong-link one? The answer would help define our hiring strategy, as well as our training and development agenda.

It's an old truism about leaders, something leaders often forget. And it is this: People won't care about how much you know until they know how much you care.

***Show you care.** Have a heart.*

Being Human

You've probably heard of Dr Apoorva Shah. He is the founder and CEO of Richfeel, and he is arguably India's best-known hair doctor.

I first met the Doc when I was working on a book about Indian entrepreneurs. As I got to know him better, I was struck by the fierce loyalty and pride that his employees displayed. I was astonished to discover, for instance, that his first seventy employees were still around, after all these years. Even his driver and cook have been with him for a few decades now. And as I wondered what the secret might be, the Doc told me the story of an accountant who worked with Richfeel.

Several years ago, the accountant had betrayed the trust of his employer and siphoned off a few lakh rupees. When the fraud came to light, the Doc did not sack him. He merely reprimanded him, and gave him a second chance! 'He is still with us, and doing well,' said the Doc. And then came the telling message: 'When someone in the family makes a mistake, you correct him. You don't throw him out of the house, do you?'

Wow, I thought. You wouldn't hear of this happening in too many modern professional companies, would you? Several leaders talk about treating employees like family. True. But when the rubber meets the road, do businesses actually treat employees as family? Does that happen in the harsh, real world of business?

The idea of employees as family comes back to my mind every time I read about layoffs. It hurts to see companies letting go of people. Not because they are non-performers, but because profit pressures are compelling leaders to cut spends and downsize organizations.

That got me thinking. Is there another way to manage these crises? If employees were indeed treated like family, what would companies do? What can they do? Is there another way, a better way?

Yes, it would seem so. For starters, leaders should hear the story of Bob Chapman. Bob was the CEO of Barry-Wehmiller, a US$2 billion manufacturing company. Not much may have been known about Bob and his company had Simon Sinek not spoken and written about him. And when Simon speaks, the world listens.

The story goes that in the economic downturn of 2008, Barry-Wehmiller was in trouble. Sales had slowed down. Margins were under pressure. And with the order book shrinking by almost 30 per cent, the outlook was rather bleak. The board advised the CEO to slash headcount and look at cost savings. They mandated a reduction in manpower, targeting cost savings of $10 million. And guess what Bob, the CEO, did? He refused to lay off people.

His reasoning was rather simple. How can you let go of an employee, just like that? Why should a man struggle to put food on the table simply because a company is unable to meet its profit projections? Bob said to his board that he saw his employees as heart count, not headcount. And that made all the difference.

So what did Bob do? He came up with a furlough plan, whereby every employee—from CEO to secretary—would take four weeks' unpaid leave in the year. In a memo to the team, Bob explained that it was better that 'we all suffer a little rather than a few of us suffer a lot'. The move worked. Employees bought into the idea. Even in a period of apparent stress for the business, the morale went up. The company saved more than the targeted $10 million. And Bob Chapman showed that 'truly human leadership' can work.

Maybe all those looking at reducing headcount and laying off employees should take a leaf out of Barry-Wehmiller's book. It might sound too idealistic, unreal even, but as Bob Chapman writes in his book *Everybody Matters,* there is tremendous power in caring for your people like they are family. If leaders like Dr Shah and Bob Chapman can do it, maybe other leaders should do it too. Treat employees like family. In good times and bad.

The time to look at improving employee engagement is not when you need employees to show they care for the company. It is when they need you to show that the company cares for them. Great leaders put people before profit to build robust businesses. Great leaders see employees as family. They think heart count, not headcount.

Become that kind of leader.

> Treat employees like family. In good times and bad. 'When someone in the family makes a mistake, you correct him. You don't throw him out of the house, do you?' Think heart count, not headcount.

One of my first mentors was a man called John. He taught me to sell. He taught me to lead. But more than that, he taught me what great organizations are all about. And what culture really means.

He also inspired me to be a 'John' to young colleagues who joined my team.

He taught me to ***do it right. And teach the right things too.***

Who Picks Up the Tab?

If you are lucky, one of the best things that can happen to you early in your career is getting a good boss. Someone who guides you, teaches you and helps you become a better leader. And a better person.

I was lucky. As a young management trainee in Hindustan Lever, my first boss was a man called John Aravamuthan. John was over six feet tall. Broad shoulders too. And that should give you a sense of how, even today, I picture him as a larger-than-life figure. He would often joke that he got hired at HLL for his ability to arrange packs of Surf on the top shelves of retail stores. And that already tells you a bit about the man. A fabulous street-smart sales guy. And so confident and self-assured that he could laugh at himself. Easily. He had joined the company as a front-line salesman and risen up the ranks. Even as more MBAs came into leadership roles at HLL, John held his own and climbed up the ladder. Learning. Growing the business. And helping others grow too.

There were many lessons I learnt from John. About sales. About leadership. And about life itself. Lessons that have stayed with me to this day and made me a bit better than I might have otherwise been.

One lesson that I often recall came out of a dinner we had at a hotel in Salem. I was training as a sales officer. And Salem, a town somewhere in the centre of Tamil Nadu, was where we had a sales depot. John had come on a 'contact visit' to meet his young management trainee. We spent the day visiting shampoo-sellers in the busy market in Salem. We then spent time reconciling promotion spends in the warehouse, like good sales officers should. And at the end of the day, we headed off to enjoy a meal together.

I recall we picked a restaurant with a dimly lit outdoor garden. A typically salesman-friendly place it was, the kind of place that had tables strewn far apart to ensure no one was eavesdropping. You could talk about the hush-hush new launch without your competitor listening in. It was a place where the entire sales team could get together. Move a few tables, get some chairs and the scene was set for a fun evening to celebrate last month's performance. It was the most popular restaurant in town at that time. But as I think about it, no better than a 2.5 rating if it was on Zomato today.

Being the 'HLL sales guys' meant we were treated well. A young lad would be assigned to wait at our table. He would scamper up and down, and make sure our meal had everything we had asked for. The extra papad, free, came with a nod of the head. And when the bill arrived at the end of our meal, I jostled to pick it up to pay, as a young boy might on his first date. Now, we were both part of the same team, same company. So, in effect, it didn't matter who picked up the tab. The company would, in any case, be paying for the meal. But as the Salem boy whom John had come to meet, I thought it was only fair that I should play the perfect host and pick up the tab. 'It doesn't make a difference. I will take it,' I said to John.

'No, no,' said John, his tone becoming a bit more measured. 'It makes a difference.'

He pulled out his wallet, checked the bill one more time and then put a wad of notes on the uniquely south Indian bowl of saunf and sugar crystals.

Then, he continued, 'Remember this. The bill is always paid by the senior-most person in the group. It's not about hierarchy. It's about the principle. Both of us will end up charging it to the company. But if you claim it, I will be the one approving the expense. Which in effect will mean that I am approving the spend on my own dinner. That's not correct. When I pay the bill and claim the expense, my boss, who is not part of this dinner meeting, approves. And that is how it should be.'

In that moment, in the darkness of an outdoor restaurant in Tamil Nadu, I could see I had received a masterclass. A simple lesson that reinforced the importance of financial integrity. The rule about no manager approving his own expenses seemed simple enough. But it was the underlying principle that mattered.

It was also a reminder that small things matter. Get the small things right, and you will never have to worry about the big things. The amount on the bill was insignificant, but not the lesson. And that was the reason why John felt it was important for his young trainee to learn the lesson. It's not the amount that matters. It's the principle. Always. Start making exceptions for small things, and you open doors for bigger mistakes.

It's now many, many years since we had that dinner. But every time I hear of a corporate scandal, or of CEO misdemeanours, I am reminded of that dinner. And of John. I can't help thinking, if only more people had the benefit of having a John Aravamuthan as coach and mentor early in their lives. They would have learnt lessons that would have kept them out of trouble. They would have learnt that integrity is non-negotiable. That you are a trustee of the organization's funds. That you are a role model to younger colleagues. And that you are answerable, always answerable, to someone else.

Unilever is often regarded as a fabulous CEO factory, a terrific school for leaders. You learn sales and marketing there, sure. As well as financial discipline and operational efficiency. And innovation and corporate social responsibility too. But most importantly, you learn the right values. Values that you live by for the rest of your life.

For me, that dinner in Salem was also a reminder of what made organizations great, and of how culture was built in an organization. No, it's not built by charismatic CEOs or wordy HR policies. Culture is created by the John Aravamuthans out there. People who embody the values of the organization, do the right things and make sure new entrants in the system learn what's right. People who take pains to explain why things are done the way they are. The world needs more leaders—nay, teachers—like John. And more great institutions like Unilever. To inculcate values in their young managers.

Thank you, John, for that lovely dinner that night. And for the unforgettable lesson too.

> Culture is created by the John Aravamuthans out there. People who embody the values of the organization, do the right things and make sure new entrants in the system learn what's right. People who take pains to explain why things are done the way they are. And inculcate values in their young managers.

Looking at the future of businesses and organizations, here's what Pat Lencioni predicts: 'Not finance. Not strategy. Not technology. Teamwork will be the ultimate competitive advantage.'

As a leader, your ability to ***make teamwork work*** *will be key to achieving terrific results. What do you do when you see sharp elbows in your team? Tolerate them—or ignore them—because of their other skills? Or pull them up (and out) because of the damage they do the rest of the team?*

How do you create a culture where everyone takes accountability for the common good?

Culture and the Kumble–Dhoni Effect

Everyone knows culture is an important part of organizations and teams. When organizations are doing well, everyone wants to understand the culture there. And when they are failing, fingers are often pointed at the organization's culture. But what exactly culture is and how you can shape it, remain shrouded in mystery.

Many years ago, Peter Drucker famously said, 'Culture eats strategy for breakfast!' That statement has helped focus attention on the importance of culture. Strategy is important, of course. Talent too. But without the right culture in place, results can be hard to achieve. What, then, should leaders do—or not do—to shape the culture of an organization?

Professors Whitaker and Gruenter have done a lot of work on culture. Here's something they have found that could offer us some clues to creating the right culture. 'The culture of an organization is shaped by the worst behaviour a leader is willing to tolerate,' they say. Look at an organization, any organization. Do you find arrogance, disrespect for other people, selfishness? If you do, chances are there's a leader out there who is allowing such behaviour to flourish. Good leaders don't let that happen. They pull out the red card when they see inappropriate behaviour.

Paddy Upton, a sought-after international cricket coach, has an interesting story to share. This is about his time as the mental conditioning coach of the Indian cricket team. The year was 2008. The Indian team was an all-star team, with Tendulkar, Dravid, Laxman, Ganguly and Sehwag. Anil Kumble was the captain of the Test team. This was a team of stars. But there was a problem, a problem often referred to in India as the 'late *lateef*' problem. Cricketers were often late. For team meetings. For practice. For the team bus departure too. Some members weren't sticking to agreed timings, and were holding up or delaying the rest of the team. This meant that the people who were on time would feel let down and irritated. Because their time was being wasted.

Picture this. It's 8.15 a.m. The team bus is ready and waiting at the entrance of the hotel to take the players to the ground. The scheduled departure time is 8.15 a.m. Everyone is in the bus. Everyone, except one player. Some days it would be one star, other days another. But the end result was that the team was often late leaving the hotel. They would reach the ground late. The net session would get curtailed. And that often meant one batsman did not get a hit in the nets.

Captain Kumble figured this wasn't right, and that he needed to do something about it. He tried talking to the individuals concerned. At team meetings, he reiterated the need for everyone to be on time. But none of it seemed to have the desired effect. That was when Kumble had an idea.

He came up with a penalty scheme. Anyone who was late for a meeting, a net session or for the team bus departure, would have to cough up a fine of Rs 10,000.

It worked. Being mindful of the penalty, players began to be on time—or even well ahead of time. You might think Rs 10,000 is not a big sum for a cricketer, but no one likes to be penalized. Players started to report on time. But only for a while. A few weeks later, one of the big boys was late. He apologized. He explained it wasn't his fault—the elevator did not stop on his hotel floor for a long time. But he had to pay up.

A few days later, another player was late. And very soon it was back to the old ways. Some player or the other would again be holding up the entire team.

The Test series ended and the one-dayers began. M.S. Dhoni was now in charge as the captain of the limited-overs team. At the pre-series team meeting, they talked about strategy and tactics. And about each man's role. Before the meeting ended, Dhoni said, 'Oh, and one more thing!' He talked of how the latecomer problem had not quite gone away, and it had not been helping the team. He talked of the penalty scheme that Anil Bhai had introduced, wherein anyone who was late had to pay up a fine of Rs 10,000. It wasn't working. Dhoni then announced that he was making a slight change to that plan. From now on, if a player—any player—was late, each member of the team would have to pay a fine of Rs 10,000. Poof!

Yes, you heard that right. If a player was late, everyone would have to pay up Rs 10,000. It worked. Like magic. And no one was ever late again. The old rule of having to pay a penalty of Rs 10,000 for being late hurt the player, sure. More the ego than the purse perhaps. But they wouldn't want to be late if that meant hurting the entire team. Getting the entire team to pay a fine, for their mistake, was a burden no player was willing to bear. People were on time. Every time.

If you think about it, that's what happens in truly great teams. Every individual feels the pain. Everyone shares the responsibility for the collective outcome. And leaders are quick to call out unproductive behaviour. They focus on ensuring the team is getting better. In great teams, individuals feel bad about letting down their colleagues. Result? Members of the team hold each other accountable and to a higher standard of performance.

If you are looking to inculcate a winning culture within your team, look no further. Follow the Kumble–Dhoni formula, and it will help you in creating a winning team culture.

First, identify specific examples of bad behaviour that the team has come to accept as normal. Actions that are rationalized as 'that's the way we are'. Behaviour that isn't helping the team's cause. Behaviour that is setting the wrong example for the younger folks in the team. Call out those behaviours, and put a stop to it. Don't worry about who's doing it. It could be another leader or a senior member of the team. But if the behaviour is detrimental to the team's cause, you need to put an end to it. As a leader, that's your job. Be a Kumble.

And second, unleash the Dhoni magic. Make sure everyone feels the pain. Ensure that everyone takes responsibility for the collective outcome. It's not enough for individuals to say, 'But I did my bit.' Magic happens when everyone takes responsibility for shared outcomes. Magic happens when every individual constantly raises the bar. Magic happens when individuals feel bad about letting the team down. When excuses go out of the window. And ownership and responsibility take a seat at the table.

When that happens, culture begins to take shape.

Great teams are like that. Every individual feels the pain. Everyone shares the responsibility for the collective outcome. And leaders are quick to call out unproductive behaviour. Unleash the Dhoni magic. Find your own version of the Rs 10,000 penalty.

Inside organizations—and inside our heads—is a constant battle: Who vs What.

In a discussion, the focus is more often on proving who is right, rather than finding out what is right.

When things go wrong, the first response is to figure out who did it, rather than what happened.

Good leaders make sure that their teams ***focus on the what, rather than on the who.***

The Man with the Golden Helmet

Even if you are not an art lover, you have probably heard of Rembrandt. This seventeenth-century Dutch master was one of the all-time-great artists. He is right up there alongside Picasso, Van Gogh and Leonardo da Vinci. For many years, a visit to Berlin was considered to be incomplete without a visit to the Berlin museum where the big attraction was a painting by Rembrandt called *The Man with the Golden Helmet*. It is a fabulous oil-on-canvas rendition of—yes, you guessed right—a man wearing a shiny golden helmet.

The museum attracted huge crowds from around the world. Everyone rushed to see that painting. Homes around the world had replica posters of the man with the golden helmet. Outside the museum, mementos with that iconic painting sold like hot cakes. Refrigerator magnets, postcards, keychains, the works. Rembrandt's *Man with the Golden Helmet* was the equivalent of the *Mona Lisa*. It didn't matter whether you understood art—it was the one painting everyone wanted to see and admire.

And then something happened.

In 1985, art experts made an announcement that astounded art lovers. They announced that they had studied *The Man with the Golden Helmet* in great detail. And their investigation had led them to the conclusion that it had not been painted by Rembrandt. It was perhaps someone else in his circle, they were not sure. But they could say with conviction that it was not the work of Rembrandt. Guess what happened next.

The crowds at the museum began to thin. Visitors were no longer interested in *The Man with the Golden Helmet*. Sales of postcards and posters plummeted. And no one remembers, or cares much about, that once-revered work of art.

The painting did not change. It was still the same masterpiece. It was just that the question 'Who painted it?' now evoked a different answer. It wasn't the great Rembrandt any more. A work of art that had long been admired suddenly ceased to seem attractive. Not because the painting changed, but because the name of the painter did.

Interesting, no?

If you think about it, the man with the golden helmet is still alive and kicking in organizations. Ideas get evaluated not based on how good they are, but based on whose idea it is. And leaders need to be aware of the danger this might pose.

The leader announces a new initiative. It's his or her big idea for the business. Everyone's talking about how wonderful the idea is, and how it will transform the business and grow revenues. Posters across locations and screensavers on desktops remind everyone of the theme. It's the boss's idea after all.

Then, as it sometimes happens, the leader leaves the organization. And his ideas and initiatives are immediately junked as strategy takes a whole new turn. What happened? Ah, there's a new painter in town!

Team meetings, too, are witness to the problem of the man with the golden helmet. The rookie sales manager's ideas are treated with disdain. But the same idea coming from the marketing director is marvelled at. We are all guilty of allowing the 'Who' to trump the 'What'—to the detriment of the organization.

Those replica posters of *The Man with the Golden Helmet* may have stopped selling many years ago. But modern-day organizations should all put up one of those posters on their walls. As a reminder that ideas need to be evaluated on merit—not on the basis of whose idea it is.

Time, then, to forget the 'Who' and appreciate the 'What'.

> The man with the golden helmet is still alive and kicking in organizations. Ideas get evaluated not based on how good they are, but based on whose idea it is. We are all guilty of allowing the 'Who' to trump the 'What'—to the detriment of the organization.

I love what they often say about values: It's not what you do when everyone is looking; it's what you do when no one is looking.

Ah, ***the value of values!***

And a good test of your values is not your answer to the question, 'What will you do when that big moment of temptation comes?' It lies in the answer to the question, 'What did you do the last time there was that teeny-weeny temptation?'

Get those small challenges out of the way. Consistently. Without fail. And the big challenges will take care of themselves.

When the Traffic Light Turns Red

'What do you do when you see a red light at the traffic signal?'

That's a question I often ask young corporate leaders and B-school students. And their answer is the same. Consistent, and quick. They all say, 'We stop.' I am guessing that was your response too. When we see a red light, we stop. That's it. Seems pretty straightforward. Everyone knows that is the right thing to do.

But it does not end there. Let us dwell a bit longer on the question. Can you think of situations when you don't necessarily stop at the red light? You can, right? Everyone I pose this question to is quick to come up with those instances. Instances where they don't stop when the traffic light is red.

Like, if it's late in the night. Or if there's no cop around. Or if it's a medical emergency, and you are rushing to the hospital. Or sometimes we jump the red light because we see everyone else is doing it too.

This is so interesting. The initial response is always, 'We stop when we see a red light.' No question about it.

But that response quickly makes way for a set of responses that suggest we are okay not stopping when the light is red. There are many, many situations when we don't stop at the red light. We all know that the right thing to do is to stop when you see a red light. And yet, we find ourselves not doing the right thing.

This brings me to the next question. If you found you could steal a million dollars—or two—from the company you work at, would you do it? Would you?

The answer from everyone is the same. A vehement 'no'. No way. Wouldn't do that. Never. And I am guessing that was your response too. You would never do that, would you?

But think again about the red light. What if it was the middle of the night and you were all alone? Would you do it? What if there was a medical emergency, and you needed the money? What if the CFO—or the cop—wasn't around? What if everyone else was putting their hands in the till? Would you do it?

No, we all say. No, no, never.

Makes me think. We've all heard of good, intelligent people who got into trouble for doing silly things at work. Like fudging expense statements. Or embezzling funds. Or insider trading. Why did they do it?

Truth is, none of us went to college or business school to go to jail. Our friends and family are all very proud of who we are and what we do. They would hate to see us in trouble—sacked, disgraced or, God forbid, in jail. Why do some of us succumb to temptation then?

The problem might actually lie at the traffic light. We should all learn to stop when we see a red light. We all know what the right thing to do is. But we make exceptions to the rule. We rationalize, thinking that it's all right sometimes. If we think it's okay to jump the red light at 2 a.m., it soon leads us to thinking that we can jump the red light at 1 a.m. too. After all, not much of a difference. And then, what's good for 1 a.m. becomes good for midnight. And then for 11 p.m. And 9 p.m. in winter begins to feel like 11 p.m. We soon find ourselves jumping the red light with impunity at all hours.

No one decides all of a sudden to rob a million bucks. It usually starts small. It seems harmless. And then it balloons into a catastrophe that destroys reputations, careers, lives even. Don't let it happen to you. The secret is simple. Next time you see a red light, stop. It doesn't matter what time it is. It doesn't matter whether anyone is looking. And it doesn't matter who else is jumping it. Just stop. Getting it right at the traffic light can help you get it right in life too.

Listen to what the late Professor Clayton Christensen of Harvard Business School had to say: 'It is easier to hold your principles 100 per cent of the time than it is to hold them 95 per cent of the time.' Yes, you read that right. Sounds counterintuitive, but it's true. Because 98 per cent soon becomes 95 per cent, which then becomes 90, 80, 70 per cent. Before you know it, you have quickly slid down a slippery slope.

If it is something you should not be doing, don't do it. Don't rationalize, thinking that it's okay. Don't fool yourself saying it is only this one time.

Holding fast to your values is quite simple really. Next time you see a red light, just stop.

You will, won't you?

> When you see a red light at the traffic signal, stop. Just stop. Remember, 'It is easier to hold your principles 100 per cent of the time than it is to hold them 95 per cent of the time.'

LEADING CHANGE

Imagine you've just been elevated to a leadership position, perhaps with a new team. Or you've switched jobs and landed a plum leadership role. And you are all excited.

Being a new leader is never easy. You want to make an impact, show you are the boss, make changes.

It's a slippery road. And you can get it horribly wrong.

Maybe you should create a wallpaper on your phone with the following message: ***'It's not about me. It's about them.'***

The Headlights in the Morning

Sometimes simple, everyday events can get us thinking and teach us valuable lessons. That was what happened as I drove my car one early morning.

It was 6.15 a.m., a little before sunrise, when I got into the car and set out. The light seemed good, so I didn't feel the need to turn on the headlights. As I drove on to the main road and stepped on the accelerator, I noticed something strange. Many of the oncoming cars had their headlights on. I wondered why those drivers had the headlights on when there seemed to be enough light.

And then, the wife offered an explanation. 'These must be people who left home much, much earlier,' she said. 'They would have started their journeys while it was still dark.' Made sense. They must have been driving for a while, and they needed the lights. I thought the visibility was okay. But by their reckoning, the visibility was okay only because they had their lights on. And I thought they must be looking at my car and wondering, 'Why isn't he turning on his headlights?'

Has this happened with you too? Were you the one with the lights on? Or were you the one wondering why the other guy hadn't turned on his headlights? I am guessing this plays out often on the streets across our cities.

If you think about it, it's a scene that also plays out across organizations every time a new leader comes in. He sees the world differently from the way the rest of the organization sees things. The new leader charges in, confident that he doesn't need the headlights. Coming from the outside, he thinks the light is okay. No need to turn on the headlights. And then he sees the rest of the organization driving with their lights on.

What happens next? A familiar script plays out. The new leader uses every opportunity he can to talk about how everyone is driving with their lights on. 'Why is everyone driving with the lights on?' That's the recurring rhetorical question from the leader. In team meetings, in cafeteria conversations and in debrief notes to his boss. He can see the problem. He can see the urgent need for change! And all the time, his team is wondering, 'Why is the new boss not switching on his car's headlights?'

So if you are a new leader moving into a new role or a new organization, hit the pause button. Good idea to remember the headlights story. It could teach you four simple lessons that can help you gain acceptance and help you settle in better in your new role.

Remember these four things. One, before suggesting someone else needs to change, ask yourself if you are the one who needs to change. Is the light good enough? Or are you overestimating how bright it is? Could it be that you are the one who needs to turn on the lights?

Two, show empathy for the other guys. Remember, our behaviour is influenced by our experience. We are influenced by where we are coming from. In our minds, we are right. We don't like it when we are told we are doing the wrong thing.

Three, give it time. In a while, they will notice that the light has got better, and they will turn off the headlights. Someone only needs to say, 'Wow, it's a wonderful, bright morning!' And good drivers usually get the hint.

And four, as a new leader, focus on the vitals, the essentials. Not on trivia. It doesn't matter if some drivers have their headlights on for a bit longer than necessary, so long as they are driving safe and headed in the right direction.

Remember that, and enjoy the drive as a new leader.

Four lessons for the new leader: One, before suggesting someone else needs to change, ask yourself if you are the one who needs to change. Two, show empathy for the other guys. Three, give it time. And four, focus on the essentials, not on trivia. Remember the headlights.

Change is hard. Changing an old habit is even harder.

We cling to the past. We refuse to let go. We are comfortable with the old, familiar ways. And it shuts the door on new ideas, new experiences. We tell ourselves what we have is the best, not because it is the best, but because we haven't seen anything better. And something better is usually just ahead, around the corner, waiting for you.

Let go. ***Don't get stuck in the past. Embrace change.*** *Say hello to the new.*

The Best Nail Clipper in the World

It was Sunday morning, and I was looking to clip my nails. After a shower, I went to get my nail clipper. It's a rather old one, but I swear it's the best! I wouldn't exchange it for any other clipper in the world. It has been with me for several years. And I have held on to it even as the wife and the kids have tempted me with new-fangled alternatives. I have often felt that my nail clipper has built a special relationship with my hands and feet. It is almost like it knows my fingers and toes very well.

As I looked around in the drawer that Sunday morning, I couldn't find the nail clipper. That trusted old favourite was nowhere to be found. The wife offered a shining new one—the one she used—but I was in no mood to give it a try. The hunt for the old nail clipper continued for the next couple of days, but by that time I really needed to clip my nails. Desperately.

Left with no choice, I reluctantly took up the wife's offer and decided to use the new nail clipper. I was apprehensive. I braced myself for an uncomfortable nail-cutting session and a painful couple of days thereafter.

But surprise, surprise. I discovered that the new nail clipper did a fabulous job. I must admit, it was a whole lot better than my old faithful. In that moment I knew I was hooked and was unlikely to go back to the old nail clipper. My fingers and toes never felt so good!

And that got me thinking.

We all have our own versions of the old favourite nail clipper. Something we cling on to—and refuse to let go of—even though a better alternative may be available. It may be a habit, a process or a way of working. We are convinced our methods are the best in the world and are reluctant to look at new ways. We resist change. And as a result, we are content with the old way and miss out on what could have been a better alternative.

Without even giving a new idea a fair chance, we conclude that our existing method is better. We rationalize that it is the best, or that it's the only one that works for us.

We are not always lucky. The old nail clipper doesn't go missing—so we don't get to experience the newer, better alternative. Or sometimes, by the time it goes missing, it's already too late.

A good idea, then, to throw away the old nail clipper. Embrace the new. Don't get emotionally attached to an idea or a way of working. Be willing to experiment. Look out for new ways to solve old problems. Your method may have served you well for a long time, but that does not mean it's still the best way to do something. The world is changing. Technology is changing the way everything gets done. And individuals and organizations need to be ready to change too. As Marshall Goldsmith likes to say, 'What got you here, won't get you there.'

Sometimes, losing the old nail clipper could be the best thing to happen to you. Better still, don't wait. Do yourself a favour.

Throw away the old nail clipper.

> We get stuck with old habits, familiar processes and ways of working. We are convinced our methods are the best in the world and are reluctant to look at new ways. We resist change. As a result, we are content with the old way and miss out on what could have been a better alternative. Good idea to embrace the new.

Stories are all around us. We only need to look. Life lessons are staring at us, waiting to be noticed. So it's a good idea to occasionally close your eyes and think of what's happening in the world around you. What do you see? Maybe use a second lens to see what the world can teach us about life, about us.

That was what happened one day as I sat in the chair in the dentist's clinic. You could argue I had no choice but to shut my eyes—given my mouth was wide open. And thinking about the world was a good distraction to take your mind off the uneasiness and pain in your mouth.

It's not that I learnt anything earth-shattering. Just that ***less is more****.*

Advice from the Dentist

My dentist is quite a chatty person. A visit to his clinic follows a typical pattern. There's me, lying on that pushback chair, mouth wide open and unable to speak. And there's my dentist, going chatter-chatter-chatter as he gets to work. One day I was at his clinic for a routine check-up. And he said something that stayed with me, long after the minty taste of the mouthwash was gone.

He was talking about the merits of rinsing your mouth thoroughly. 'Take some water into your mouth and do a nice squish-squish. It works like magic,' he said. He then mentioned how a lot of his patients listen to him—and then get it all wrong. In their eagerness to do a good rinse, they take too much water into their mouth. Result? They are unable to create the force needed to propel the water around inside the mouth. Less water is better; it allows for more manoeuvrability and leaves room for us to create those little jets that do a thorough cleaning job. For the water to work, it needs that little extra space. Too much water has the opposite effect. Less is more, said the good doctor.

Interesting, I thought. And I couldn't help thinking how that advice might be useful not only for dental hygiene but for our lives too.

Looking to give performance feedback? Aiming to help a friend get better? The 'less is more' principle holds true here too. In our eagerness to change other people's behaviour, we make the mistake of pointing out too many things we want to see changed. We are keen to see dramatic results, so we don't miss a minor point even. Result? The hapless person doesn't know where to begin. He is unsure which changes are the most important and ends up confused. And we are disappointed when we don't see the change we were looking for. Good coaches know this. To get the best results, they focus on the single biggest driver of change and get the coachee to work on it. One change, implemented well, beats a twenty-point change agenda. One change is easy to work on. The twenty-point agenda gets talked about but is seldom implemented. When you aim for one change, you allow yourself to focus all your effort and time on making that one change happen. That is powerful.

I remember my first days on the driving range at the local golf club. I hit the ball all over the place and after every shot, my caddy-turned-coach would point out what I was doing wrong. Keep your head down. Move your hands closer. Hold it tight. Then hold it loose. Move faster . . . The list of instructions seemed never-ending. And as you might guess, my game didn't really improve. Until a good coaching professional came along. He watched me hit, didn't say a word and then, after a while, suggested one change. Just one change. He altered my grip. I focused on that, relaxed a bit, and the change was quite dramatic.

Here's another thought. Next time you are trying to help a colleague accomplish a task, don't spell out every little step of how they should do it. Leave room for them to use their imagination and creativity to complete the job. Leaders often get too caught up with their own knowledge and experience. And they ask their colleagues to 'do exactly as I tell you'. That's a sure-fire recipe for a disengaged employee. Tell them what to do—and explain why they might want to do it. And then watch the magic happen.

> Remember, to rinse your mouth well, you must take in less water, not more. Next time you are working at getting better—or helping someone else get better—remember the dentist's advice. Less is more.
>
> One change, implemented well, beats a twenty-point change agenda. One change is easy to work on. The twenty-point agenda gets talked about but is seldom implemented. When you aim for one change, you allow yourself to focus all your effort and your time on making that one change happen. That is powerful.

There's a print ad campaign from the '50s that is often touted as one of the finest pieces of advertising. It was the 'Think Small' series of ads for the Volkswagen Beetle. It sold a lot of cars. And it also provided the best advice you can get to manage change and improvement—advice that, in many ways, paraphrases the principles of Kaizen that have become universally popular.

A mistake we can all make when we are down—or looking to improve our lot—is to look for that one big, revolutionary idea that will change everything. Small ideas, tiny changes don't excite us. We don't think much of them because we don't see any real change happening because of those small tweaks. We are in search of that magic bullet. Which doesn't exist.

Small, consistent changes work like magic. The power of compounding begins to work in your favour. Never underestimate the power of small changes.

The Volkswagen Beetle guys were right. **Think small.**

The Power of 1 Per Cent

The year was 2002.

Great Britain had always prided itself on its sporting culture. Despite its relatively small size, it had been among the top performers in the Olympic Games. They had done well across sports. Except cycling. In eighty years of competing in the Olympics, they had won just one gold medal in cycling. Not good enough, they reckoned. And they decided to do something about it.

To drive the change, they brought in Dave Brailsford as the director of cycling. And they gave him a simple mandate: Make Britain a champion nation in cycling. Create champions. Win golds.

People who knew Dave often referred to him as the one-per-cent man. His philosophy was simple. Working on a huge task or a big challenge? All you need to do is break it up into tiny bits, sub-tasks, and get to work on making each of those tiny bits a little bit better. One per cent better. When you put all those improved bits together, the results are quite astonishing. Work on small improvements and marginal gains, and the end result could be a big, big difference. So if cycling is what you are looking to get better at, here's what Dave would recommend. Break down everything you can think of that goes into riding a bike. Improve each of those by 1 per cent. And you will get a significant increase when you put them all together.

So what did he do? He changed the angle of the bicycle seat, to make it more comfortable for each rider. He changed the fabric used for their cycling jerseys, so they would sweat less. He hired a doctor to teach the cyclists how to wash their hands. Why? To make sure they were germ-free, thereby reducing the chances of illness and ensuring they were fit on race day. He even changed the pillows the cyclists slept on. The new pillows were chosen to ensure that the cyclists had a comfortable night's sleep before the race. And those pillows travelled all around the world with them. The motto was 'think small', not 'think big'. Think improvement, not perfection.

Result? Those teeny-weeny 1 per cent improvements worked. Like magic. Britain won seven out of the ten gold medals in cycling at the Beijing Olympics in 2008. Now, if someone told you that to win gold medals in cycling you should change the pillows, you would have laughed. But strange things happen. Nothing is too small. Or insignificant. Everything counts.

What worked for Britain could work for you and me too. In our organizations and in our lives. Making small, seemingly insignificant changes can make a huge difference in results. Faced with a major challenge, we all tend to look for that one big idea, that magic bullet, that can change our fortunes. Truth is, the magic bullet seldom exists.

Better to focus on small improvements. All those 1 per cent things. Things that we can all do. If you can do a hundred of those 1 per cent improvements—the results are bound to show.

Small, consistent change can be powerful. As James Clear explains in his must-read book *Atomic Habits*, small changes can alter our lives. If you get better by 1 per cent every day—just 1 per cent better—by the end of the year you would be thirty-seven times as good as you were on day one. Imagine. That's the power of small, consistent improvements.

Great organizations and great performers are obsessed with the idea of continuous improvement. They are working to get better. All the time. They have an obsession with making those small changes that can help them get just a bit better. Get that obsession.

What are you working on? What are your 1 per cent improvement opportunities? Don't wait for a big transformational idea to get better. Get to work on the small stuff.

Sometimes, a better pillow can help make you a cycling champion. Find that pillow. Fast!

Working on a huge task or a big challenge? All you need to do is break it up into tiny bits, sub-tasks, and get to work on making each of those tiny bits a little bit better. One per cent better. When you then put all those improved bits together, the results will be quite astonishing.

Walking inside a retail store with Kishore Biyani, I learnt a valuable lesson from the man widely regarded as the raja of Indian retailing. I was suggesting that Big Bazaar, catering for the masses, shouldn't necessarily look too shabby. We should be looking to add a bit of shine and polish, and spruce it up a bit.

And KB responded: 'When you walk with your customer, you should make sure you stay only one step ahead. Lead the way. But be available to hold his hand, and make sure he is comfortable. Never go so far ahead that you have no idea where your customer is, what problems he is experiencing and he doesn't feel he can reach out to you for help.'

That's terrific advice for retailers. And for leaders too. ***Stay close to your team.***

Who's Afraid of the Escalator?

As I walked towards the escalator at the Mumbai airport, I saw something I had seen a few times before. An elderly man was standing at the edge of the escalator, staring nervously at it. You could tell, here was someone who had never stepped on an escalator before. Some folks accompanying him were trying to cajole him to take that first step. One of them got on to the escalator, to show how easy it was. Another voice—I should have checked the sneakers she was wearing—screamed, 'Just do it!' But that man stood there transfixed, watching the steps on the escalator running away from him.

Sounds familiar? I am guessing you have witnessed this scene. Somewhere. Sometime.

As I later took my seat in the aircraft, the image of the man struggling to get on to the escalator flashed back in my mind. I thought about him. About the escalator. About his nervousness and struggle to step on to it. And then it struck me. In many ways, that escalator moment exemplifies the challenges leaders face every day.

As a leader, you know there is a better way to do things—and the escalator represents that. The better way. Left to themselves, people might prefer using the staircase and doing things in the old familiar way. But it is the leader's duty to help point his team towards a better way, and help the team traverse that path. In most cases, the leader himself may have 'been there, done that'. He has been on an escalator before, sure. He knows it is better. But the leader also knows it's not about him. It's about his team. The real challenge is to make sure his team gets there too.

And the man standing nervously at the edge of the escalator? He represents the folks in your team. How does your team feel about walking on the path you've set for them? They are not sure they know how to do it. They are scared they will fail. And often, they are too scared to ask for help.

You should freeze that image of the 'escalator moment' in your mind. It might help remind you of the simple things you need to do to make sure you become an effective leader. So how can you make sure you get it right?

First, recognize that while you may know what it takes to get to the goal, your team might not. Don't assume your team knows it. They are usually at a different place on the learning curve. You've been on that escalator before but your team has not.

Second, make it easy for your team to say 'I don't know'. Make sure they are not scared to ask for help. They should not have to fear that they are not good enough.

As a leader, how do you make it easy for other people to ask for help? Simple. Talk about your own vulnerability. About your own apprehensions the first time you stepped on an escalator. And about how you overcame those fears. Next time there's something you don't know, be willing to ask for help. Good leaders are comfortable saying 'I don't know'. That's at the heart of an organization that is learning. That's also the hallmark of good leaders.

Third, when a person is looking for help, how do you respond? Do you show your surprise at his incompetence? Or do you lend a helping hand? In fact, how *did* you respond the last time someone asked for help? Did you jump on the escalator and say 'Hey, look, it's so easy'? Did you show off how good you were at riding on an escalator? Or did you acknowledge their fear and show them how it was done? When that nervous colleague is staring at the escalator, it's not the best time for you to exhibit your escalator-riding skills. If he's looking for help, that's all you need to offer him. Help.

And finally, don't rest content with the notion that 'it doesn't matter how they do it—so long as the job gets done'. Don't leave them to use the stairs. Don't rationalize that you don't care how they get there as long as they do get there. Escalators beat staircases. Any day. And as a leader, it is your job to make sure you help your team get on to the escalator.

Years later, when your colleagues look back on their lives, what will they remember? They won't care about how the stock price climbed during your leadership. They would have forgotten how many points of market share they gained under your watch. But chances are, they will fondly remember a leader who helped them learn to ride the escalator. A man who taught them to embrace the new and who helped them reach their destination faster.

Be that kind of leader.

Freeze that image of the 'escalator moment' in your mind. It might help remind you of the simple things you need to do to make sure you are an effective leader. Recognize that while you may know what it takes to get to the goal, your team might not. Make it easy for your team to say 'I don't know'. When a person is looking for help, just help. Don't rest content with the notion that 'it doesn't matter how they do it—so long as the job gets done'.

I have had a problem with my sneakers. And I am wondering if you have experienced something similar too.

I had a new pair of expensive walking shoes. Good-looking, comfortable. But the damn laces would keep coming undone. I would walk a bit and then suddenly discover that those round, smooth nylon laces that I had carefully tied into a knot had gone loose.

Happened to you? Yes? Ah, I am feeling good already.

So good, in fact, that I want to share some lessons I learnt from those shoelaces. About ***leading change****.*

Tying My Shoelaces

The morning walk with the wife is a ritual I enjoy and quite look forward to. And I want to tell you about the time I bought myself an expensive pair of new sports shoes. A good-looking pair it was. And you can imagine my excitement as I set out for the walk in my new footwear the next day.

About twenty minutes into the walk, though, one of my shoelaces came undone. As I stopped to tie the laces, I didn't think too much about it. But when it happened a second time I sensed that there might be a problem. I suspected the problem was with those rounded, smooth nylon laces in my new shoes. Have you faced a similar problem at some time? Ah, good to hear.

The shoelaces coming undone soon became a regular, recurring phenomenon. The wife and I would be walking along, talking about the day gone by and the day ahead. And then I would discover that my laces had come undone. I would find myself interrupting the flow of the conversation—and the walk—to tie my shoelaces.

I began to wonder why the Nike folks couldn't provide better laces, given the high price I had paid for the shoes. I even thought of writing to the CEO to share my predicament. Meanwhile, I could sense my wife's irritation mounting too. I sat there on the road, tying my shoelaces yet again. And I could bet she was thinking, 'Why couldn't his parents teach him to tie his shoelaces right?'

I was determined to set it right and yet unsure of what I should do. I decided to do what all curious thinkers do when they aren't sure of something and need to find the answers. I Googled it. 'How to tie your shoelaces?' Bingo!

Google quickly enlightened me that there are, in fact, two ways of tying shoelaces. Similar in technique but different in outcomes. The start is straightforward enough. You make a loop out of one end of the lace and hold it. You then get the other end around it. And here lies the rub. It makes a huge difference whether you bring the other end from above the first loop or from below it. Bring it from above and you have a weak knot. But bring it from below and you will have a knot that's strong. There is a weak knot, and there is a strong knot. As it turned out, I had, all along, been tying the weak knot. Damn.

Armed with this new knowledge, I began to use the technique to tie my shoelaces the strong-knot way. And it worked.

No more interruptions in the walk. The laces stayed in place. And as a bonus, I now had a delighted wife too. I could see her smiling with pride. Delighted that at this ripe old age, her husband had finally mastered an essential life skill.

The shoelace problem is out of the way now. But the lessons have remained, and they are relevant for us all.

First, just because you have been doing something for years, it does not mean you have been doing it right. Get that. There could be a better way. You need to be willing to learn. It doesn't matter how many years you have been doing something if you have been doing it wrong.

Second, when things go wrong, the temptation to blame others can be strong. Shoelaces coming undone? It must be Nike's fault! It's the smooth round texture of the laces. It takes courage to introspect and say that maybe, just maybe, the fault lies within. Own the problem, and you'll empower yourself to find a solution.

Third, change is hard. Doing things in a different way is harder than it seems. At work and in life, we all get used to a process, a pattern of work. Habits get formed, and they are hard to change. Acknowledge that. Change takes effort, as well as time and commitment.

Finally, it's useful to remember that small changes can make a big impact. A simple thing like getting the lace from above the loop—or below it—can make a huge difference. It can keep your shoes on your feet. Heck, it an even bring a smile to your wife's face.

So next time you are looking to drive a change initiative in your organization, think of the shoelace. If you need to make a behavioural change and get better, think of the shoelace.

Skip the blame game. Take ownership. Start small. See if there is a better way. Recognize that change is hard. Then, as the change kicks in, get ready for the appreciation.

Just because you have been doing something for years, it does not mean you have been doing it right. Get that. There could be a better way. When things go wrong, resist the temptation to blame others. Change is hard. Doing things in a different way is harder than it seems. And remember, small changes can make a big impact.

'And'.

It's a word that aptly sums up what being a leader really entails. It's not about choosing between two seemingly conflicting objectives—but finding ways to deliver on both. It's not about increasing sales or increasing profit; it's doing both. Not about being task-oriented or people-friendly. It's both.

Good leaders learn to live with that. A sense of urgency is nice to have. But patience is a skill too. Sometimes our quest for results can cause us to go overboard, and things can go horribly wrong thereafter.

A bias for action. And patience. *Maybe that's a good set of traits to have.*

Turning the Ship

On a holiday some years ago, we went on a sunset cruise on the picturesque Lake Balaton in Hungary. It might have remained just another boat ride had it not been for an interesting conversation with the captain of the ship.

We were in the middle of the lake. The waters were calm. People began to strike up a conversation with the captain. Some of the children on board were getting pictures clicked with him. And some of the grown-ups were getting their hands on the ship's steering wheel, getting that feeling of being in command of the ship. I did that too and soon found myself in conversation with the captain. With my hands on the wheel and the captain by my side, I asked him about his adventures at sea, and the stories began to flow. He interrupted the conversation and said to me, 'Turn left!'

I did as I was told and turned the wheel. That was easy, too easy. The ship continued to go straight. So I turned the wheel to the left one more time. But nothing happened. So I turned the wheel once more. And that was when the captain said to me, 'Wait, wait! Not so much. Turn a little. And wait for the results.' And then I remembered it takes a long time to turn a large ship. 'If you keep turning, it will be too much, and the ship will go way off course,' said the captain.

Wow, I thought to myself, as I reflected later on those words from the captain. *Turn a little. Wait for the results.* That's terrific advice—no matter whether it's a ship you are at the helm of, or a team or business. Do what you need to do. And then wait for the results.

We have all been guilty, at some time or other, of being impatient for results. We have seen start-ups flounder because they spent too much, too soon. The business idea was terrific. But they were desperate to scale up quickly. And when those high-growth numbers didn't happen as planned, they lost their way.

Large companies have seen great product launches fizzle out. The product was good, the strategy was right. But the launch sales targets were way too high. With the projections not materializing, the marketing teams got impatient. They ended up discounting the brand too much in the trade to meet those unreal sales targets.

We do the right things first, but when we don't see the results, we get impatient—and make mistakes. We overdo things. We mess up.

An edtech entrepreneur once shared an interesting insight about what makes start-ups fail. He said it is not because they don't have a good idea. Nor is it because they do not execute well. They fail because they don't correctly estimate the time it takes to succeed. Investors get impatient. Targets are missed. And a great idea and sound execution get waylaid. His advice? Be patient. If you think it will take you three years to be successful, add three more. Prepare for the long haul.

Take a look at any list of leadership competencies or success factors. You will usually find phrases like 'sense of urgency' and 'drive for results'. Seldom, if ever, will you find 'patience' in the list of those virtues. Patience and its cousin perseverance are both underrated. In our frenzied dash to the finish line, there seems to be little time for good, old-fashioned patience.

There are other problems, too, that can arise out of a leader's impatience. Team morale, for instance. You tell a teammate what needs to be done. But even before he gets a chance to do it and show results, you get impatient. You remind him. You check on him. You tell him how to do it. You are at the poor chap's throat, not giving him a chance to breathe, telling him the same thing again and again. Then, in a classic case of leadership failure, you do his job because you can't wait.

Plants don't grow twice as fast if you give them twice the amount of water and extra manure. They take their time to grow. And that's true for businesses and people too. Good to remember that you might have the right medicine to cure the ailment, but an overdose can kill. A sense of urgency is good to have. Leaders must make things happen fast. But not faster. Patience can be a leader's best friend!

Next time you feel things aren't moving, remember the captain's words. Turn a little. Wait for the results.

We do the right things first, but when we don't see the results, we get impatient—and make mistakes. We overdo things. We mess up. Good to remember that you might have the right medicine to cure the ailment, but an overdose can kill. Turn a little. Wait for the results.

One of the biggest challenges for a new leader is driving the change agenda.

You are keen to stamp your imprint on the team and the organization. You can see lots of stuff that you want to change. Everywhere you turn, you see opportunities for improvement. You quickly think of what you did in your previous organization. And in private conversations you say that you can't understand how the team could be doing these things here.

Be careful. Be very, very careful. Before wielding the broom and implementing sweeping changes, think a bit. Why did they do it this way? Surely, they were not all fools. ***Understand and appreciate where they are, before blindly forcing the change.*** *Do you understand how challenging it might be to do it your way, under new circumstances? Unless you get that, your change agenda will most likely fail. And unfortunately, so will you.*

When You Can't Understand Why!

Have you heard of Chesterton's fence? It's an interesting concept and a powerful lesson that can help us think differently about driving change in our lives. The term owes its origin to the author G.K. Chesterton, who first wrote about it in his book entitled *The Thing*.

Chesterton talks about a town where a fence has been constructed across a road. A modern reformer comes into town, sees the fence and says, 'I don't see the use of this fence; let us clear it away.' Hearing this, a wise old man says to him: 'If you don't see the use of it, I won't let you clear it away. Go away and think. Then, when you can come back and tell me that you do see the use of it, I may allow you to destroy it.' That, then, is the essence of the concept. You shouldn't get rid of a fence until you've understood why it was there in the first place.

If you are a reformer, it is a good idea to remember that the fence did not magically come up from the ground one day. It wasn't as if it some idiot put up the fence in a fit of madness. Whoever built the fence did it because they felt it would serve a purpose. There must have been a reason. The reason may not be relevant anymore. That's possible. But we need to understand the rationale—before deciding to do away with the fence.

If you've seen a leadership change in your organization, you would have seen Chesterton's fence. A new leader takes charge, and change becomes the dominant theme. Hardly a day passes without the new leader getting rid of the 'old ways of doing things'. Policies get changed, strategies altered, roles disbanded. And the new leader is on his way to putting his stamp on the organization. Change is good, no doubt. But reckless change can sometimes cause more harm than good. If it's not thought through, reform can turn into deform.

'I don't know why we have so many branch locations,' says the new leader as she goes about shutting down those offices. Might be the right thing to do. But before deciding to do away with them, it would be a good idea to pause, and understand why those branches came into existence in the first place. Shutting those offices might be the right action, who knows. But thinking about why the branch offices were set up will help. It will prompt the leader to think about how they will serve customers in all those remote locations.

Being aware of Chesterton's fence helps us in two ways. First, it ensures that you have thought through the consequences, beyond the obvious, before you take action. Often, we are convinced of the merits of our actions, and disregard the consequences and possibilities someone else might have thought of. 'I don't understand why it's there' is not a good enough reason to get rid of it.

Understand why it is there, seek out answers, and then you'll be better placed to decide whether or not it should be there.

And here is the second benefit of keeping Chesterton's fence in mind. It teaches you to respect your predecessors and their decisions. You may disagree with them, but remember, they weren't stupid. Times have changed, but there was a reason why they did what they did. Understand that.

Go ahead, then. Change the world. But do remember Chesterton's fence.

> 'I don't understand why it's there' is not a good enough reason to get rid of something. Understand why it is there, seek out answers, and then you'll be better placed to decide whether or not it should be there. Respect your predecessors and their decisions. You may disagree with them, but remember, they weren't stupid.

One of the most powerful motivational quotes from the world of sport is this line from Michael Jordan: 'I've missed more than 9000 shots in my career. I've lost almost 300 games. Twenty-six times, I've been trusted to take the game-winning shot and missed. I've failed over and over and over again in my life. And that is why I succeed.'

If you've never failed, you probably haven't yet discovered what you are truly capable of. ***You haven't really become a winner until you have failed.*** *It's a good idea to get comfortable with failing.*

Next time you think of the hundred centuries Sachin Tendulkar scored in Tests and One Day Internationals, remember another number: thirty-four. That's the number of ducks against his name. Thirty-four times, the world's greatest batsman got out without scoring.

It happens. Winners fail. And they are okay with that.

The Fosbury Flop

Sports on television is big business. But unfortunately, it is a handful of sports that capture all the eyeballs. And all the sponsorship money too. Football and cricket. Tennis. And now kabaddi too. Athletics—sport in its purest form—gets some attention, but only during the Olympics.

I have always found high jump fascinating. I remember watching, wide-eyed, the seniors at my school doing the jump. I could never do it. And that only added to its mystique.

You may not know too much about high jump and world records. And you may not care. But there are two lessons we can all learn from that sport, lessons that can help us succeed in our lives.

For the first lesson, let's flashback to 1968. Remember Dick Fosbury? He won the gold at the Olympic Games in Mexico that year. But that's not his real claim to fame. Fosbury was the man whose technique changed the way athletes jumped over the bar. Before Fosbury, this was how they did it: the athletes ran straight in and came face to face with the bar; they then jumped over the bar, their feet crossing it first, and their body and head following. Fosbury did the opposite. The exact opposite. He ran towards the bar, turned his back to it disdainfully and then launched himself over the bar, head first. People watching could hardly believe what they saw. It looked odd. Weird. But it worked. And today, every jumper does what's come to be known as the 'Fosbury flop'.

We should all be doing it too. In our lives and in our work. Sometimes, a problem can seem difficult to solve. A challenge can appear daunting. When that happens, it is a good idea to change the way you go about trying to crack it. Do the unusual. Defy the norm. Are you only doing what everyone else does? Only doing what you've always done? Time to try a different approach. If you always jumped feet first, time to explore a head-first technique. It does not matter what your line of business is. It does not matter how successful you've been in the past. Think of Fosbury and try something different. Think different. Do different. And yes, get ready for the applause. That's lesson one.

For lesson two, let's take a quick look at the format of the high jump event. Every competitor gets three tries to clear the bar. If they are successful in clearing it, the bar is raised, and they get to take another shot at it. If they can't clear it on three attempts, they get knocked out. The elimination continues till there are fewer people left after each round. Until there are three, then two, and finally one—the winner. Does it stop there? No, it doesn't. Even after the winner has been identified, the bar gets raised again, and the winner jumps to see if he can clear the bar. If he succeeds, the bar gets raised again, and again, until he tries and fails for three attempts.

High jump is not about seeing who can jump the highest. It's also about seeing how high the finest athlete can jump. And it's an event where the winner has to fail—before he is declared the winner.

Now that's a fabulous lesson for us all. You aren't the winner until you've failed! Winning in high jump—as indeed in business and in life—is not about being better than the other guy. It's about being the best you can be. It's about going beyond and testing yourself to see how good you can be. It's a good mindset to adopt, a mindset that urges you—nay, compels you—to strive for excellence. That's the real mindset of a champion. They know that 'good is not enough if better is possible'. High jump teaches us that we have to fail in order to win. It tells us that we need to push ourselves, and our teams, not only to beat the others but also to be the best we can be.

Too often, we are scared to fail. We hesitate to attempt something we are not sure we would be successful at. We play safe. True champions get comfortable with failure. They know it's okay to fail. A loss is never the end of the world. Try till you fail. Push yourself till it hurts. Stretch your limits, or else you will never know how good you might have been.

Being a winner in life is simple. Think like a high jumper. Keep your eyes on the hurdle, on the challenge ahead. Believe in your ability to jump over the bar, to overcome. But after every success, raise the bar. Dare to think differently. Do the Fosbury flop.

And yes, one more thing. Remember, you aren't a winner until you have failed.

> Two lessons from high jump, for success in life. One, think of Fosbury and try something different. Think differently. Do something different. And two, you haven't won until you've failed! Winning in high jump, and indeed in life, is not about being better than the other guy. It's about being the best you can be.

WHAT REALLY MATTERS

The pandemic has changed our world in many, many ways. The loss and suffering that so many people have endured have also been unthinkable. It's a time that has challenged leaders to up their game. To overcome adversity. To innovate. To think differently.

It's also been a time that has required leaders to show some kindness. Kindness wasn't always a word associated with leadership. But in our changed world, kindness has become a defining trait of a good leader— nay, of all of us. We've sought love and care. And when we've shown some kindness, we've made other people feel better. And we've felt better too.

We used to think we could dazzle people with our intellect. We liked to show how much we know. And we didn't really worry about things like caring for our people.

Until now. But all that has changed. The rules of the game have changed.

***Show kindness. Show you care.** Learn to give. Learn to share.*

The world needs it. Your team needs it. Show some love today, won't you?

The Magic of Giving

It happened in the early days of the lockdown, in April 2020. A time when economic activity had come to a sudden standstill and daily wage earners were struggling to make ends meet. A friend's NGO got into the act and started to supply food packets to those affected. And the wife decided to help with raising money to support their efforts.

One morning, she was busy making calls to friends and family, telling them about the plight of daily wage earners and about the friend's NGO that was helping them. She asked them to contribute to what was a good cause. As she put the phone down, something interesting happened. Our maid—who has lived with us for two decades—came up to my wife and gave her a hundred rupees. It was her contribution to help those in need. We were touched. And it brought home a universal truth. Giving has nothing to do with how much you have. It's about wanting to give, wanting to help other people.

Most of us get caught up in our own worlds, and we have no time for other people. Giving, then, does not come easy. We tell ourselves, 'When I become a millionaire, I will give away 10 per cent.' Truth is, if you cannot give away Rs 100 today, you will find it impossible to give away Rs 100,000 later in life.

As I thought about it, I was reminded of a lesson from the world's richest man: Jeff Bezos, the founder of Amazon. Bezos once shared an interesting little story from his childhood. This was while delivering the commencement address to Princeton's class of 2010. He talked about the time when he was ten years old and on a road trip with his grandparents. His grandfather was driving, with his grandmother sitting in front. She smoked all through the journey, and Jeff hated the smell.

Sitting on the back seat, he recalled seeing an ad on TV, about how every cigarette puff took away two minutes of your life. As a kid who enjoyed puzzles and mental maths, he did the numbers in his head for his grandmother. Cigarettes per day. Days in a year. Years she would live. Two minutes per cigarette. There! He knew he had found the right answer. With pride filling that ten-year-old chest, he leaned forward and announced, 'Grandma! At two minutes per puff, you've taken nine years off your life.' He thought his grandparents would be proud of his maths wizardry. He thought they would pat him on the back. But something strange happened. His grandmother began to cry.

His grandfather pulled over and got off the car. He then got young Jeff out too, and the youngster wondered what was coming next. His grandfather said to him: 'Jeff, one day you'll understand that it's harder to be kind than to be clever.' And those words stayed with Bezos. As he went on to explain to the students at Princeton, cleverness is a gift, kindness is a choice. Gifts are easy. Choices are tough. Our lives are all about the choices we make.

As our maid's gesture reminded us, Bezos's lesson is one we all need to take to heart. We spend most of our lives trying to be clever, not kind. It's harder to be kind than clever. And guess what? It's more satisfying too.

Remember, giving is a mindset, an attitude. It has nothing to do with how much you have. Giving a little can bring us all more joy than what we may experience with having a lot. Try it.

Be kind. Discover the joy of giving.

> It's harder to be kind than to be clever. Be kind. Discover the joy of giving. And remember, giving has nothing to do with how much you have.

Well begun is half done. We have all heard about the importance of getting started. Making a strong beginning is key.

But learning to finish is a terrific skill to have. Just learning to close out, complete tasks can be a source of joy—and can fill us with a sense of accomplishment too.

Stumbling at the last hurdle is a risk we all run. Remember, there are no prizes for almost getting there. Don't get complacent. Don't take your foot off the pedal.

Unfinished tasks are a source of great stress. You've got started, you've done the hard work, and now just a bit is left. But it never seems to get done.

***Stay focused. Be a finisher.** Tell yourself it is just one more step. One last step. Get it done.*

And get ready to pop the champagne. After the last step.

Not before.

The Last Step

I walked down the steps, all twenty of them. Then I thought I was on level ground. But I wasn't. There was one more step. The last step. And I almost fell as my foot went searching for the level ground it thought it had reached.

Has that happened to you too?

You are climbing down a staircase. You are careful. You are in control. And then, when you think you are done, bang. You falter. At that last step.

We all need to be careful about that one last step. As they say in sports, it isn't over until it is over.

Made me think. Doesn't something like this happen in our lives too? We think we are done, but in reality we are still short. We think we've reached the finishing post, and stumble before getting there.

Remember the game between India and Bangladesh in the 2016 T20 World Cup? When you think about individuals or teams stumbling in the end, it's hard to not think of that game. India made 146 for 7 in their 20 overs. And in reply, Bangladesh did well. With six balls left, needed 11 runs with three wickets in hand. They managed 9 runs off the first three and needed 2 more runs. Off three balls. With three wickets remaining. Easy. The batsmen were pumped up. Their teammates in the dugout were preparing to celebrate a famous win.

And they lost a game they should have won, losing three wickets off the last three balls.

What happened with Bangladesh, happens to us all. With the end in sight, it is tempting to let your concentration waver. You get a bit ahead of yourself. You are already savouring what success feels like. But it's not done. Not yet.

Almost getting there is not the same as getting there. Remember to pay special attention in the end. There are indeed many a slip between the cup and the lip. When success is near, it can look deceptively closer than it is. Watch out for that.

And yes, next time you are climbing down the stairs, mind that last step.

> We all need to be careful about that one last step. As they say in sport, it isn't over until it is over.

At the end of the game, both the king and the pawn end up in the same box. No one cares which was the bigger piece or the more powerful one. But people will remember what the king and the pawn did while the game was on.

Our lives are like that too. The idea is not to live forever, but to leave behind something that will.

***What's your legacy?** What will people be saying about you when it's all over?*

Remember this. When that great Scorer puts your name down, he won't see whether you won or lost—but how you played the game.

What's Your Legacy?

Imagine.

The year is 2050 AD. After a long and successful career, you've recently hung up your boots. What's your leadership legacy going to be? What will people be saying about you? What stories would they be telling other people about you? A former boss of mine once mentioned an interesting question that kept recurring in his head. 'I often wonder,' he would say, 'When I am seventy years old, who will want to have coffee with me?'

Back to the present then. What is your legacy going to be? Have you ever thought about it? What happens once that awesome-sounding designation gets prefixed with 'ex'? Who among your colleagues and associates will want to have coffee with you? What will your friends and family be saying about you?

The problem for most of us is that we are preoccupied with the here and now. We are busy meeting this month's target. Delivering this quarter's numbers. Making sure we meet that project deadline. We have little time to think about stuff like long-term impact. Let alone airy-fairy ideas like leaving a legacy. Unfortunately, those target-busting, record-setting performances are soon forgotten. The focus shifts to next month. Next quarter. Next project.

Great folks are remembered for the legacies they leave behind. So how can you create your own legacy? Here are five pointers—five conscious choices we can all make—to help you build a lasting legacy by the year 2035.

1. Strive for significance, not just success

We are all driven by a need for achievement. We strive for success. It sure is nice to get a fancy title, a large car and a fat bank balance. But it's unlikely that you will be remembered for any of those. Focus instead on significance, on making a difference. Impact the people you work with. Help them get better. Show them you care. Make them feel valued. Make your world a better place. You weren't just meant to do a job. You are here to make a difference. Make it count.

2. It's about them, not me

We spend a lot of time worrying about our own performance, our achievements. All of which is useful during annual appraisals but of little relevance in the context of a legacy. Because legacies are not about what you achieved—but about the impact you had on other people. Turn the spotlight away from yourself, towards the people you work with. James M. Kouzes and Barry Z. Posner got it bang on in their book *A Leader's Legacy*: 'It's not about how big a campfire you built, but how well you kept others warm.' Think about that.

3. Work on it now, don't leave it for later

Most of us think of legacy-making only at the end of our careers. That's too late. Your best chance to create a legacy is now. Not later. Legacy-creation opportunities come up every day, right from the start of your career. Grab them. Or else you will look back and say, 'I should have.' Or, 'I could have.' Don't wait for the day when you become CEO to start thinking about your legacy. Legacies are built over a lifetime and not as a hasty postscript to your corporate career. You've created plans for the business. You've planned your career. Now start thinking about your legacy too.

4. Strive for work–life balance, in your legacy too

Everything you know about being effective at work, apply that to your life too. Make a business plan for your life. Invest in relationships. Think long-term. Worry about your stakeholders—your wife, kids, parents, friends, society. Think of the spouse as your customer. Never take her for granted. Do the small things that delight her. Go the extra mile. In short, make your life your business. It is nobody else's business anyway.

5. People remember stories, not numbers

Leaders deliver results, sure. But they also do story-worthy things through their lifetimes. That brash young management trainee you hired from campus. What would he be saying was the biggest lesson he learnt from you? And that coffee boy in the Chennai branch office—what story would he remember you by? Heck, would he remember you at all? When it's all done and dusted, people won't be talking about your market-share gains and sales-growth numbers. They will be telling stories about the kind of person you were, the things you did and the difference you made. The numbers will be forgotten, the stories will remain. What's your story?

Think of it like this. We all have two buckets in our lives. One is the CV bucket and the other is our legacy bucket. The secret is to remember to fill both.

We spend the best years of our lives working hard, achieving more, making more money, building our careers and becoming successful. We slog to make our personal brand more valuable.

Our focus is on filling the CV bucket.

Then, at the end of our careers, we find a reasonably full CV bucket. And we wonder why it hasn't made us happy.

Maybe we should focus on filling the legacy bucket too. Do stuff that makes a difference to the world we live in, impact the people closest to us. Be a good friend, colleague, spouse, parent, sibling. In the end, that's what really matters.

Think about it. When your innings is over, and you are dead and gone, what will they be saying about you? No one ever says, 'He was such a fine man. He had two apartments in South Mumbai.' Or, 'She got promoted to

VP faster than the rest of her batch.' No, no, nobody ever says that.

People will talk about how good a friend you were. What a loving and kind human being you were. And how you made the world a better place, with your laughter and compassion.

There's an old Chinese proverb that says, 'The best time to plant a tree was twenty years ago; the second-best time is now.' Legacies are like those trees. You would wish you had started working on your legacy twenty years ago.

Luckily, 2050 is still some distance away. But like objects in the rear-view mirror, it's closer than you think. Now is a good time to start thinking of your legacy. Make a beginning. Make a difference. Touch a life. Teach. Care. Give. Show some love.

Time, then, to focus on the legacy bucket too. It's never too late.

Your time starts now.

> When your innings is over, and you are dead and gone, what will they be saying about you? No one ever says, 'He was such a fine man. He had two apartments in South Mumbai.' Or, 'She got promoted to VP faster than the rest of her batch.' No, no, nobody ever says that.
>
> They will talk about how good a friend you were. What a loving and kind human being you were. And how you made the world a better place, with your laughter and compassion.